JOHN   FROM   MAUREEN + JOHN   003

CW00544605

The Second Meadow

By the same author

Fiction
A Corridor of Mirrors
Sergeant Sahib
Prison Bars

Non-fiction
A Cage of Shadows
Closed World of Love
Summer's End

Juvenile fiction
Dark Pastures

Archie Hill

The Second Meadow

Hutchinson
London Melbourne Sydney Auckland Johannesburg

Hutchinson & Co. (Publishers) Ltd

An imprint of the Hutchinson Publishing Group

17–21 Conway Street, London W1P 6JD

Hutchinson Group (Australia) Pty Ltd
30–32 Cremorne Street, Richmond South, Victoria 3121
PO Box 151, Broadway, New South Wales 2007

Hutchinson Group (NZ) Ltd
32–34 View Road, PO Box 40-086, Glenfield, Auckland 10

Hutchinson Group (SA) Pty Ltd
PO Box 337, Bergvlei 2012, South Africa

First published 1982
© Archie Hill 1982

Set in VIP Meridien by
D. P. Media Limited, Hitchin, Hertfordshire

Printed in Great Britain by The Anchor Press Ltd
and bound by Wm Brendon & Son Ltd,
both of Tiptree, Essex

British Library Cataloguing in Publication Data

Hill, Archie
  The second meadow.
  1. Hill, Archie
  I. Title
  941.082′092′4   HV248.H447

  ISBN 0 09 147570 8

This small book
is for Wendy

Acknowledgements

The author and publisher gratefully acknowledge the following for permission to quote material: the estate of the author and Secker & Warburg Ltd for the lines from James Elroy Flecker's 'To a Poet a Thousand Years Hence'; the estate of the author and Macmillan and Co. Ltd for the lines from Ralph Hodgson's 'Time, You Old Gipsy Man'; the estate of the author and Jonathan Cape Ltd for the lines from Robert Frost's 'Stopping by Woods on a Snowy Evening'; the author and Cassell & Co. for the lines from Robert Graves's 'To Bring the Dead to Life'.

To see a World in a Grain of Sand,
    And a Heaven in a Wild Flower,
Hold Infinity in the palm of your hand,
    And Eternity in an hour.

William Blake, *Auguries of Innocence*

The Second Meadow

One

I thought he hadn't seen me, but he had. He waited for me on the fringe of the woods, almost completely blended in with the surroundings. He wore camouflage jacket and trousers, like army battle issue, the trouser ends tucked into stout leather lace-up boots which came halfway up his legs. The floppy-brimmed hat he wore looked like ex-army issue, too, as mine was: a 'jungle hat'.

He held a double-barrelled shotgun in the crook of his left arm, the gun broken at the breech for safety, the twin muzzles pointing groundwards. As I drew nearer to him I could make out his features more distinctly, could see the leather-coloured and textured skin of his face and hands, the sun and wind weather lines round his eyes and mouth. I placed his age in the middle sixties, the clue being in his face and not in his body. His body looked as lithe and fit as that of a young man in his thirties. I was panting with exertion as I dropped my burdens in front of him and nodded a greeting.

'You're Mr Hill, I take it?' he asked, his voice a mixture of Worcestershire burr and Staffordshire clippedness. I croaked agreement, trying to get my breath back.

'My name's Turner,' he said. 'I'm the head gamekeeper to the estate. His Lordship up at the house told me to watch for you – you, er, a personal friend of his, sir?'

I didn't want to get onto familiar terms with Mr Turner so I ignored the question. To get familiar with the gamekeeper or anyone else for that matter would defeat my object, which was to have no direct contact with any human being other than myself for three months.

'If you'll just explain the lie of the land, Mr Turner,' I murmured politely, 'then I won't keep you from your work. I'll sort my things out and settle in.'

He eyed me doubtfully.

'Aye, then,' he said at last, 'leave your things there for a while and step with me. I'll point the way of the land to you.'

I followed him in silence round the edge of the wood, finally up a steep incline where I could see out over meadows and pastureland where cattle were grazing. Beyond the fields were more woodlands, shading away into the mist-wraithed blue distance. I stood alongside the keeper as he pointed out the salient features to me.

'The Big House is just beyond that coppice,' he explained, 'and my cottage is half a mile beyond that. The woods behind us, where you left your stuff, cover nigh on two hundred acres. Bist that enough space for you, sir?'

'Plenty. That's enough room to stretch in.'

'Going to live in a tent, bisn't you?'

'Yes.'

'Weather's apt to be a bit unpredictable this time o' year for camping, bisn't it, sir? How long you reckon on staying?'

'Three months.'

He shrugged, a rather-you-than-me sort of gesture. He pointed towards the hazy west.

'Yonder's Shropshire,' he said. 'When the mist lifts, you can see the Wrekin. 'Bout thirty miles away. Birmingham's a step or two farther to the north. Redditch and Bromsgrove bist around ten miles off from here – your nearest main towns. Stourbridge is the first town you'll come to if you step over the county border into Staffordshire, an' that's eighteen, twenty miles off. But happen you won't be up and out to visit the towns?'

I shook my head, no.

'You'll be shooting to fill your cooking pot, then. What's the gun you're carrying?'

16

I unslung it from my shoulder, took it from its waterproof scabbard and showed it to him.

'Single shot,' I explained. 'An air rifle.'

He chuckled. 'Won't get much by way of that,' he said patronizingly. 'A boy's thing is an air rifle. Ain't you got no shotgun?'

'This one will do me. It's powerful, it's accurate. And it's quiet.'

He took the rifle from me, examined it critically. He hefted it in his right hand, setting his own piece carefully on the ground to do so.

'Got a nice weight and balance to it,' he admitted at last. He brought the butt up to his shoulder, squinted through the eyepiece. 'Not a bad telescopic sight, either. M'mm, not bad at all.' He handed the rifle back to me, picked up his own gun.

'Still a kid's plinking toy,' he muttered. 'No power to 'em. You'll be going hungry, sir, if you have to rely on this to fill your pot. 'Specially with summer gone and autumn getting its winter woollies out'n its cupboard.'

I was immediately on the defensive, protecting the virtues of my rifle. 'It equals or betters your shotgun for range,' I told him firmly. 'It'll kill a sitting rabbit at over forty yards with a head shot. I've shot many a one with this rifle.'

'Ah, a *sitting* rabbit. Bet you'd miss, though, if the rabbit were running. *My* gun wouldn't miss.'

I was almost glaring at him. 'How *could* you miss? With two barrels full of spread shot? Takes more shooting skill to drop small game with a single shot such as mine.' His eyes were amused, as if he were listening to the bleat-boastings of a small child. 'Yes, sir. Of course, sir. You know best.'

I could imagine him next time he went into his local ale-house for a pint, telling his cronies about 'the city chap hoping to fill his cooking pot with a toy gun'. And his cronies laughing their heads off with him and refilling his glass as a reward for his funny story. He'd probably get free drinks for a week, I thought, on the constant repetition of his tale.

I put my rifle back into its scabbard and slung it by its strap from my shoulder.

'Right,' said Mr Turner. 'You've got two hundred acres of woods, with plenty of dead logs and kindling for your fire. Plenty o' pigeons and doves and rabbits in there, if you reckons as you can shoot 'em with that thing. The master of the Big House says you can do as you like within sensible reason, go where you want and nobody to interefere with you. Leave you alone is our orders, and that we'll do. Nobody 'ull come nigh you. You ever done any rabbit trapping wi' wire?'

I nodded a yes.

'Hast any wire with you?'

'No.'

He shook his head glumly, reprovingly. 'Should allus be prepared,' he told me. 'If you'm not prepared then you might as well arrange to have your meals sent up from the Big House.' He took a well-worn pipe from his pocket, filled it from his tobacco pouch, puffed away with contentment. Then he stabbed the pipestem in the direction of a small spinney to the south of the larger wood, about a mile and a half away.

'Just inside the tree line o' that spinney,' he explained, 'you'll find a small hidey-hut. I keep a few tools in there, spades for digging foxes from the earths and the like. It's a place I sit in betimes to study the moods of the fields and woods. I shall leave some trapping wire there for you, you can collect it when you've a mind.'

I started to thank him, but he brushed my thanks away.

'My gaffer told me you knew what you were about,' he said, 'so I'll take his and your word on that. Just remember to close gates behind you when you've passed through 'em, so's not to make my job any the harder. And watch your campfire so the flames don't get to drying out the pine needles and causing the fire to spread. You'll find a stream near where you'll be setting your tent up – there's a few fish in it if you've got the patience to hook 'em out any way you can. My orders are, you'm a free agent.'

18

Again I thanked him. He made to walk away, then paused

'There'll be a few guns about a few weeks hence,' he said, 'taking the pheasants from the big woods yonder. It's over a mile away, so the business shouldn't disturb you. There's no pheasants in your woods, except the odd passer-by. You're welcome to the odd one or two, but if you see any number of 'em you might flush 'em out for me. They'll go and join t'others, then. All right?'

I nodded. 'All right.'

'If you see any owls, magpies, jays, crows or that sort of bloody nuisance and your gun can manage 'em, you might nail the carcases to the outside of my hidey-hole from time to time. There's nails and a tacking hammer inside. Good day to you, sir. 'N' good luck.'

I walked back to where I'd left my gear. The noon sunlight was hazy but quite warm, but the early darkling evenings meant that I couldn't stand around in idle sightseeing. I had to get settled in. W. H. Davies's poem 'What is this life if, full of care, We have no time to stand and stare?' couldn't, at the moment, apply to me.

I came upon the stream part way in the woods on the western flank, the opposite side to where the Big House and keeper's cottage lay. The location I chose for pitching my tent was a fine one; in a fair-sized clearing was a gently swelling hillock, and that's where I pitched so that if it rained the water would drain away from me. It was a good spot, with no overhang of tree branches. My pup-tent was old, an army leftover from the war, USA issue, and I felt that a persistent drip-drip of rain from branches would find the chinks in its age . . . I felt it would survive general rain, but not the 'Chinese water torture'.

Having pitched, I telephoned Old Konk the poacher through my memory banks. Konk, who'd taught me the tricks of poaching and survival through my boyhood and early manhood years.

I phoned: he answered.

'Sithee, chap. Shelter first, then fuel supply, then fire and food and water. S, three F's and a W. It don' matter what order thee puts 'em in, as long as they bist all together.'

I scouted around for fallen branches, dragged them to my location, then chopped them to length with my hand axe. Even as the blade of my axe ate through the bark and meat of the branches, I felt a warmth from it. Not a heat warmth, but a thought warmth. Wood. Friend of man alive or dead, whether baked to charcoal or left to earth's pressures for millions of years to be compacted into coal. Wood's important to man, despite man invariably only regards it as an abstract commodity mostly growing wild. Yet wood's his close companion, seldom a step away from his existence. It forms the paper upon which his birth certificate is written, and the coffin in which he is buried. During his journey between the two extremes, the trees recycle the air he breathes, provide him with nuts and fruits, delicate oils and resins, properties for health-giving medicines, struts and spars for domestic roofs of home, refuge and larder for birds and wild life. Then, when it has served its thousands of purposes, man still has two final uses to make of it. Fire-glow to dream and warm himself by, and finally the ashes to plough into the soil to feed other plants yet to bloom. But wood from different trees has different properties, different quirks and characteristics, as with mankind. I wonder if that's why we refer to our own blood lineages as 'family trees'.

Beechwood gives out a clear, bright flame from the log, but oak is slower burning and the heat more intense, making for better cooking and simmering of the food pots. Outdoors, I like burning larch and pinewood logs because of their scent-smells, but both woods throw out so many sparks, spluttering and crackling, that you daren't leave them to look after themselves but have to stay in close attendance, in case they cause other, uncontrolled, fires. Birch and alder logs aren't worth the chopping, because they burn too fast – much faster than the effort it takes in cutting them up. Chestnut, elm, wild apple, cherry – all give off a good smouldering heat, and cherrywood especially is worth mixing in with other burning logs for the scent alone. Lovely, like flowers in bloom. Ash logs, in my opinion, are the best main source of campfire fuels, both for cooking heat and the warm companionship of flame. The wood in which I was to live for three months held out a promise of many assorted logs to be gathered in and mixed to any recipe I fancied.

I hacked and chopped at the logs I'd fetched in, keeping the chippings to one side for initial kindling, then graded the chopped lengths from thin to thick. I stacked the timber round the boles of nearby trees to keep it dry as possible in case rain came. Then I took my water containers to the stream and filled up. So, I'd got shelter, fuel and water. Fire and food to come. Fire first, I thought, and then check my equipment whilst it's still daylight; I can eat by firelight. My 'official' three months' sojourn didn't really start until next day, so I felt I could indulge myself a little longer. One of my problems, really. Procrastination. From boyhood, even Old Konk had always expected me to do the immediate possible.

I unpacked my trenching tool (another army leftover) which had a short strong shaft and a double steel head. One part of the head formed a small, almost pointed spade. The opposite part was a well-pointed pick. I scooped a depression from the ground with the tool, about ten feet in front of my tent flaps – enough distance to prevent the wind from blowing smoke in on me if it got up. As I'd gathered the fuel wood I'd noticed a number of largish pebbles lying around, and I fetched them. Some I laid in the depression I'd dug to make a floor to hold the heat together, and others I placed round the edges to make walls to contain the fire safely. During the next few days, I thought, I'll improve on things and make a cooking range.

I unpacked all my equipment from rucksack and kitbag, and took inventory. I'd got the clothes I was already wearing – vest, pants and socks for underwear, topped by a good thick roll-collar woollen jersey, hard-wearing Levi jeans, strong hiking boots and a waterproof anorak with hood, and

21

plenty of pockets to the garment. My spare clothing added up to two complete changes of underwear, wellington boots, an extra pair of jeans, a quilted ski suit, a couple of shirts for sleeping in in lieu of pyjamas, a jungle hat, and that was about all so far as clothing was concerned.

In a small metal box I'd got needle and thread, a few safety pins, and half a dozen surgical Band-aids. Inside the same tin were exactly a dozen red-tipped matches and four cigarette lighter flints. I'd got a full tobacco pouch to feed my pipe, and once this was used up I intended to attempt to give up smoking altogether, or experiment with wild herbs and leaves. Apart from an extra groundsheet for the tent and my sleeping bag, the tobacco and pipe were the only luxuries I'd got with me. The nearest village shop was three miles or more away – I'd left my car there, in the garage-cum-handyman's side shed, and had walked to what I already regarded as 'my wood'. I'd got my air rifle (which for some reason which escapes me I always called 'Stella', and still do) and two tins of .22 slugs containing 500 shots each. I'd also got a Toledo steel bowie knife and an all-purpose jackknife which contained, amongst other fittings, a small pair of scissors for keeping my finger and toenails clipped. For culinary use I'd got a small water container and a collapsible canvas bucket, a dixie tin set which could be used as a frying pan or, with lid on, a cooking pot; two small lightweight saucepans, one fitting inside the other, and that was that. The jackknife (a Boer War relic) had a small spoon and an eating fork attached to its sides, as well as various spikes for taking stones from horses' hooves: a challenge or task I doubted would zoom in on me. To cap it all I'd got just one simple emergency meal. An Oxo cube, a small tin of pilchards, two slices of bread wrapped in cling foil, and a nugget of cheese. These emergency rations were to be my supper for this first night, and from tomorrow onwards I'd have to fend for myself.

I repacked the supplies I'd got no immediate use for, memorizing the order in which I packed them for future reference. The kitbag and rucksack were both waterproof, which would be a blessing as the weeks went by and the weather turned lowery and damp. By the time I'd got my campfire lit the dusk was already harvesting itself across the woods and landscape. Birds were returning from their feeding grounds to take up sleep perches in the trees, rustling and grumbling and twittering as they preened their feathers for the night. I could hear pigeons roaring their low monotonous voices to each other, and the more musical cooings of the ringdoves. Tomorrow, I thought: I'll come looking for you tomorrow. In the short meantime, sleep well.

I took up a handful of axe chippings and shaved them into tiny slivers with my bowie knife, placed them in the centre of my fireplace. Around the slivers I placed a circle of small twigs, then extended the circle with larger ones, then with size-graded logs. I struck one of the matches and placed it among the wood shavings, cupped my hands round the tiny blaze until it started to spit. Gradually I teased a few small dry twigs to the flame, then more, until I could add thicker ones and, finally, slender logs. Within twenty minutes I'd got a fine fire going, hot in the centre, with other logs round the edges to dry them before it was their turn to burn. The flames spluttered and chuckled at the enclosing night, the smoke rose upwards as if seeking a hole in the darkness to pass through. I opened the can of pilchards then spread the fish and its tomato sauce onto the bread and ate it thick and spurting like an old-time navvy's 'buttie'. After I'd wolfed this down, I ate the cheese. Then I sat and smoked a pipe of tobacco, listening to the wood and night noises creeping around me on pit-a-pat feet. I sat looking at the fire, letting my mind paint pictures with the flames, as I did in long-ago childhood when there was no instant central heating . . .

Visions of childhood, stay, O stay,
Ye were so sweet and mild;
Yet distant voices seem to say
It cannot be, they fade away,
Thou art no more a child . . .

It wasn't a cold evening. Just a slight autumn nip in the dark air, warmed at the edges where it breathed upon my fire. I'd already lost track of clock time, having no wristwatch with me: I thought it best to keep in touch with calendar time at any rate, so got to my feet and searched out three strong hazel twigs. One twig for each month. Two of the twigs I tossed under the flysheet of the tent to keep them dry, and I carved a circle of bark from the third to identify it as my first month calendar stick. Starting tomorrow morning I'd cut a nick into the twig, then one nick for each passing day. After ninety such notches it would be time to pack up and go home. Precise clock time would sort itself out, as far as I was concerned, inside the motions and rhythms of Nature.

I sat by the fire a while longer, then poured water into one of the dixie tins and boiled it up. I dropped a knife-scraped chip of wood into the water so that dust and ash from the burning logs would adhere to it, held there by the water's centrifugal motion as it boiled. It was then a simple matter to lift the chip and debris out with my spoon, leaving the water clear. I popped the Oxo cube in and let it melt, built the fire up whilst the drink cooled a little. Then I sat on my log seat and sipped the drink, and it tasted good.

So to bed, I thought, and stripped down to my underpants and tee-shirt before sliding into my sleeping bag. I'd intended to sleep in one of the spare shirts I'd brought with me, but since I'd repacked them without thinking of the need, I let it go at that. The ground felt hard beneath me but I'd made a small depression for my hips to fit into before erecting the tent, so it was none too bad. I snuggled myself into a comfortable position, rucksack for pillow, and left one entrance flap of the tent slightly open so that I could see the firelight flickering. An owl scolded deep in the darkness, his territory disturbed by me, the intruder.

I lay thinking and musing on the events that had brought me to this place, the reasons and challenge. For a long time I'd wanted a change from convention, social restrictions and imprisonments – I wanted an area of time and place where I could try to be myself, whoever that might be, instead of what or who people *wanted* me to be. No, I didn't want loneliness, I wanted *alone*ness. I wanted to touch comparative freedom for a little while, shrug off domestic responsibilities, unregiment my life. The urge to find this small oasis was almost an ache, but the excuse or opportunity to ease the ache kept passing me by. It required effort to seek out that oasis, and all my efforts had hitherto been geared to bolstering up obstacles to prevent the search. Meetings to attend, writing to be completed, money to be earned for bills to be paid. The clock face of time wiping its grubby hands across my existence; habit, conformity, reliability, and creature comforts to give a pretended ease to the movements of daily routines and monotonies. I was fed up to the back teeth with breathing the same daily ration of stale air, I needed a deep gulp of difference. I was a trained talking parrot trying to get out of its cage and spread its wings for a while. That was all.

The opportunity came when we were driving back to London from Birmingham, a friend and me. I'd been to Pebble Mill Studios to give a radio talk, and felt that it hadn't gone too well. Stilted, unflowing, flat: that's how I felt about it, although the producer had seemed perfectly satisfied. This flatness of feeling, this staleness of self, had been with me for a long time, increasing in its intensity: my mind constantly felt like a mouthful of unbrushed teeth the morning after a binge. A sort of mental and spiritual constipation requiring a laxative. On the drive down, all around us, were neat orderly arrays of headlights tunnelling through darkness. White bright lances sucking the vehicles after them. Man-made comets streaking through distance at 70 m.p.h., going north, going south. Going somewhere. Big cars, little cars, trucks, lorries, coaches ripping the night into shreds with head- and spot-lamps. Here and there a high-powered vehicle snatching extra slivers of distance with illegal speeds, speedometer needles grabbing for the 100 m.p.h. plus . . . here and there a Jack Russell mini-car yapping and snarling a neurotic passageway through the three-laned traffic. Somewhere up and above the ground-mist reflection of car lights was a deep sky pinpointed with stars. Passengers like me could look out and up if they'd a mind to look at stars, but the drivers couldn't. They were wheel-and-screen-tied, machines inside machines. Driving so, I thought it would be good to turn off at the next intersection and find another road – a better road, even if not so fast ... little puppy lanes squiggling and wriggling to nowhere in particular, at their own pace, flanked with hedgerows and quiet resting places; and beyond the hedgerows open fields ever ready for the constant kiss of plough and harrow, waiting for the consummation of the scattered seeds leading inevitably to the birth yields of harvestings. Quiet, unhurried rhythms of Mother Nature.

We drove on, listening to the roar of engines, the whip-lash swish of passing wheels. Past the illuminated signposts, the emergency telephone boxes on the hard shoulder, past service centres.

'Want me to pull in at the next one and grab some coffee?' he asked me.

I shook my head, no. I didn't want to go into a smelly restaurant to sit at a plastic table on a plastic seat, sipping coffee from a plastic beaker, stirring the contents with a plastic spoon. Sit there among the smells of fried bacon and eggs, chips and toast, looking through a window watching the vehicles racing by, heavy trucks rumbling. Going north, going south, going somewhere.

'Going nowhere,' I said aloud, 'none of us. Only through motions.'

Four-wheeled, six-wheeled, twelve-wheeled worlds scurrying by. A solitary motorbike went deep-throat roaring for London, as if being reeled in by its own headlamp.

That's what my publisher friend called 'order'.

'Perfect symmetrical order,' he murmured.

'What is?'

'That. The three-laned motorways ... the straight lines of cat's-eyes. Neat, orderly and pleasing.'

My answer scolded at him. 'That's what *I* call chaos. Absolute, unadulterated chaos.'

'Why so . . . ?'

'If you claim that it's order, then you're the sort of bloke who looks at an erupting volcano and says "That's chaos."'

'So . . . ?'

'Not so. The volcano blowing its top is *order*. It's Nature, getting the phlegm off her throat.'

He chuckled. 'I see,' he said. 'You prefer Nature in the raw to the comforts of civilization – that it?'

'I'm not sure,' I replied at last. 'I don't really know.'

'Why don't you find out?'

'How?'

'Go back to Nature. Live out of her pocket for a while. There might be a new book in the offing.'

I gave it some thought for a mile or so. 'No. It's been done before.'

'But *you* haven't done it.'

I watched our headlights melting twin pathways through darkness. Going south. Going nowhere. 'How long for?'

'Say three months? Or as long as you can take it.'

'What conditions?'

'The bare necessities. No luxuries. No radio, television, newspapers. No contact with any other human beings. Live off the land and off your wits. I'd allow just one concession. Wherever you put down you can let the local police know where you are. Let your family have the police station phone number in case of emergency. That's all.'

It sounded tempting. My memory slipped down the pathways of the years, seeking men I'd known long ago when I was a boy, before the war; men who'd been forced through unemployment to poach and live by their wits off the land in order that they and their families could exist.

Old Konk . . . Konk the poacher who'd been my surrogate father, friend and God, all rolled into one. Long dead, now, but still living and breathing inside my mind. I could hear his

27

voice coming over the hill of the years, from the woods of the past.

'Go on, me lover,' I could hear him saying. 'Thee knows thee can do it.'

'I know I can do it,' I said aloud to my companion gripping the steering wheel.

He nodded, the glow from the facia board lighting up his grin. 'No cheating,' he said. 'Just you by yourself, for three months.'

So here I am, I thought drowsily before falling asleep: alone . . . by myself . . . ripping a paragraph out of my life in order to be as free as it's possible to be free . . . lines from Rupert Brooke . . . 'Known arms embraced me . . . safe at last, I slept . . .'

Two

I woke up to the early dawn chorus of chittering birds, wondering where I was. I knew even before I was fully conscious that I was in strange surroundings. A leftover reflex from my years with the armed forces abroad, a reflex so ingrained that it was permanently a part of me. Not all the senses go to sleep. At least one remains always awake through the dark watches of the night, the personal sentry guarding the mind. Strange how these military-instilled and trained habits never fade. When I come awake I never make a sound, never yawn, never open my eyes immediately. My breathing never alters from that of the rhythm of sleep. I let my ears tell me where I am, tell me if there is anyone else close to me, if everything is as it should be. My ears concentrate upon the vibrations around me, ready to recognize safety or menace upon the immediate instant. Those who know me also know that it's unwise of them to lay a hand upon me when I'm asleep, to shake me physically into wakefulness. It's a habit I can't break with. For a moment or so I lie as if still sleeping, eyes shut, breathing steadily. Then I strike out with my fist in the direction that my sentry instinct tells me to strike, then roll away from whoever it is shaking me. I've frightened one or two people by this instinctive reaction, drawing blood from one. I once struck a commissioned rank, the orderly officer, who woke me from sleep by shaking my shoulder. No charges were brought against me, since even the officer afterwards agreed he'd used a wrong method. The best way to waken a sleeping man, especially one who's been through battle training, is to rap gently on the soles of his feet. A better way, if the circumstances require the physical touching of a sleeper and complete silence is necessary, is to place a finger gently under the sleeper's earlobe, at the point of the jaw hinge, and steadily increase the pressure. The sleeper comes awake silently, fully alert and conscious, without fuss or commotion. An old trick, this, learned from the American Red Indians when they had to break camp quickly and steal silently away before the 'Blue Bellies' surprised them.

Lying so, I let my senses pinpoint myself in place and time, brush the cobwebs from my mind. Then I relaxed, warm inside my sleeping bag, staring out through the open chink of tent flaps. Sunlight was beginning to checker patterns through the leaves, making a crazy paving of light and shade across the clearing. The thought of morning coffee slipped into my mind, and with it the realization that I hadn't got any. Nor any breakfast, either. Get up and forage, Hill, I told myself, else at the end of the three months somebody's going to find your bleached skeleton lying here in the tent. I rolled out from my simple bed, shivering slightly in the morning chill. The sun hadn't built up a head of steam as yet, hadn't brought its own kettle to the simmer. I dressed quickly, jeans, woollen roll-neck jersey and – upon seeing the dew outside – my wellington boots over thick socks. I rolled the tops of my rubber boots down so that they only came halfway up my legs and wouldn't chafe. I left the tent, took a few deep breaths of morning air. The smell of pine trees touched my nostrils, sweet-acrid, exciting. I walked to the stream and splashed water over my face, feeling the prickliness of first-beard stubble under my hands. It'll soften as it grows, I thought, as the days go by and no razor scrapes at this battered middle-aged face. That was my wash for the day. Later on, I'd sort out a more thorough ablutions routine. I went back to the campsite and drank water which I'd pre-boiled the night before, then scrubbed my teeth. Toothbrush, paste and hair comb I had with me but in no way considered them to be luxuries. They were necessities.

The larder, I thought. Better get some rations in first, and then set to 'holing in' on a more or less fixed basis. Despite I'd just swilled my hands and face at the stream, I now scooped charcoal ashes from the dead fire and streaked my face and areas of exposed flesh with them to form camouflage. I knew from past experience that pigeons would be up and away from their tree perches the second they saw a white blob of face staring up at them. They'd catch the wind and ride it like the clappers of hell until they were well clear of the intruder. Two things in particular are alien to Nature and wild life: straight lines and the human form. Man has yet to learn that he's a parasite in Nature's scheme of things, and a dispensable parasite at that – increasingly so since the Industrial Revolution. Man takes all from Nature's cupboards, and never puts anything back. He's not master of Nature, and he's no longer her servant. Just an unwelcome traveller crashing through to, probably, an empty destination.

Oh well, I thought, no heavy thoughts on an empty stomach. I clipped the bowie knife to my belt, took up my rifle and leather pouch of pellets – I'd transferred them from their tin to prevent the sound of rattling going ahead of me and announcing my presence – and set off into the deeper woods against the slight wind. I carefully fastened my tent flaps first, knowing how inquisitive squirrels can be once they get to poking around. One eight-ounce bundle of curiosity can do a hundredweight's worth of damage.

I walked carefully, warily, trying to make my feet kiss the ground, no more. Heavy foot-tread vibrations would broadcast advance signals to feeding rabbits, who in turn would drum hind feet against the earth to warn their brethren to make for the safety of their buries. Hunting for the pot, especially with such a light rifle as mine, called for every care and skill which could be culled from memory and experience. And at the same time new skills were constantly being added to the old ones. A hunter's instincts couldn't merely equal the instincts of his quarry, they had to be better. They had to anticipate, be one step ahead: Kipling expressed the hunter's skill perfectly in his story of Kim, who found a missing sheep, or goat, or some such. When others who had searched for the animal but failed to find it asked Kim how *he* had found it, he answered sensibly enough: 'I just sat down and thought about where I'd be if I were a goat. Then I went to the place, and there it was.'

The swoosh-swoosh murmur of my turned-down welling-ton boots caused me to stop. The sound was alien to the woods, the small game would be put on the alert. I packed the tops of the rubber boots with grass and leaves, forming a tight pad between boots and legs. When I moved on again, the noise was gone.

That first day was easy. I shot three plump wood pigeons with clean kills inside the hour, and decided that would do for starters. But before I returned to camp with them I carefully picked up every spilled feather and put them in my pocket to burn later on when I'd got the fire going. Pigeons just won't 'come in' when there are traces of their own kind lying on the ground.

'Pigeons bisn't stupid, thee knows,' Old Konk had drilled into me long ago. 'Got eyes sharp as hawks, they have. Loose feathers on the ground makes 'em suspicious, and they won't come nigh.'

I made my way back to camp by another route through the woods, letting my eyes mark where the rabbit runs lay from the evidence of their droppings. I saw squirrels leaping across the tree branches, and in a hedgerow the smoot of what must have been a larger than average hare. I once paused at the sight of some less familiar animal droppings, and it slowly dawned on me that they were the dung fewmets of deer. I searched for slot markings (deer footprints) until I found some on a patch of bare moist earth. The slot marks were small and dainty, those of roebuck deer: Britain's smallest deer, about eighteen inches to the withers when full grown. Shy, elusive creatures – pretty in a kid's picture book, but a menace to the environment unless they are kept in check and carefully culled by gamekeepers and forestry keepers. They can do terrible damage to trees and saplings. Probably the pricket is the worst offender – he's the two-year-old buck with spiked horns and when these itch towards mature antlerhood he scrapes them against the bark of trees, going round and round until a complete circle of tree bark is worried away, and with it the death of the tree. A fully antlered buck causes the same damage and havoc when he too starts rubbing the moss from his own antlers. But I had to shrug from my thoughts the deer's presence in the woods – there was nothing I could do to provide myself with venison. My gun was too light in stopping power other than to wound them. And anyway, they were legally protected game to a large extent.

Even as I stood up from my stooping position of examining the slot marks I saw the 'target', the white rump, of a small deer disappearing into the thickets. The white target serves the same purpose as a rabbit's tail, markers to keep the animals together when they sprint from danger. The target of the disappearing deer was all that I could clearly see, the autumn coat of the small beast blending in so splendidly with the undergrowth and surroundings.

Back at the campsite I set to and carefully plucked the pigeons, then slit them from breastbone downwards and removed the entrails. Some pigeon eaters slit through to the skin, and peel skin and feathers away in a couple of clean sweeps, but this doesn't appeal to me. I like the skin to remain intact, so that it retains the flesh juices, and crisps up nicely when roasted over an open fire. I placed feathers and entrails in the fire pit, ready to be consumed when I started the flames. Before going to the stream to wash the plucked birds I remembered my calendar stick, and cut the first day's notch into it. Only eighty-nine more to go . . . dammit, I thought, I've only just arrived and I'm already thinking of going back. Am I *that* much of a conditioned slave of my time? To hell with it.

33

I took pebbles from the bed of the stream and filled the gutted cavity of each bird's belly. The weight made them too heavy to float away and I could safely leave them in the cleansing water until I was ready to cook them. My stomach was already sending out grumbling rumblings of hunger, but it would have to sing its dirge a bit longer. There was essential work to do. I took up the trenching tool and hacked out three holes from the ground. One – quite shallow – near to my tent was to be a grease pit. The other two, which I dug a goodly distance away from tent and stream, were to be my lavatories. They were quite deep when I'd finished digging, and I was sweating and panting like a jockey completing the Grand National with the horse on his back. I dug two lavatory pits simply to have one always in reserve, in case a bad spell of weather set in when one of the holes was used up and the top soil and turf replaced. 'Think upwards and sideways,' Old Konk used to tell me. 'Always plan sideways and frontways. Think on tomorrow as well as today.' Dock leaves and the like would serve as toilet tissues, after which use I would take my ablutions at a spot well downstream from the point where I drew my drinking water. A good animal never fouls his own den. I had to have a system, part of my mind insisted; I thought you'd come here to escape from systems, the other part muttered. But living off the land didn't mean ending up like a vagrant tramp, did it?

'Cleanliness is next to Godliness, lad,' Konk's ghost voice told me, 'an' while I don't give a damn who He chooses to have stand next to Him, I like clean-smelling folks next to me.'

I laid small twigs inside the grease pit, making a mental note to fashion a roof for it from plaited brambles and evergreen leaves to keep the rains out. The grease pit was a sensible innovation, really. I'm surprised every household doesn't have one, out in the back garden, to eke out the cost of kindling wood. But I suppose central heating has put an end to the need. When you boil or roast meat in a cooking pot – pigeons, squirrels, rabbits, starlings, the like – there's always

34

an amount of grease that floats to the surface. By scooping this off and pouring it over the twigs in the pit, I'd got useful firelighters for damp days. I could also, if I needed it, make a 'see-by' lamp by melting some of the grease inside one of the pellet tins, then cutting off an inch or so of bootlace and letting it float in the grease like a candlewick – it would just give enough light to see by inside the tent. I'd seen the nomad Arabs use an almost identical method when I'd served in the desert. If I wanted stronger light, I could make tallow dips from the clumps of bulrushes lining the banks of the stream.

I surveyed my three dugouts with satisfaction, drank more stream water, then took up my axe to increase my supply of fire fuel. Around me in the woods was a variety of trees, as varied as the contents of a Chinese takeaway meal. The fir tree loppings and the pine, mixed in with other woods, were ideal for both warmth-giving and perfume. A smell like joss sticks, and I could scour off the resin which the heat forced from the logs and pour it into my grease pit like a crude turpentine. I'd already given a deal of thought to the meals I'd have to seek out. Meat, fish, acorns and dandelion roots for coffee, nuts, fungi, chickweed, berries, nettles, dandelion leaves – these would be necessary to make a balanced diet. Two meals a day was my target. A light one at noon, and a more substantial one at evening. Standing five feet eleven inches, I'd weighed just on twelve stone when leaving home. I'd never tended towards fatness or overweight, but decided I could safely afford to lose a few pounds of city flab and tone myself back to the wiriness of my youth. Anyway, I'd build upon a confusion of improvements as I went along, arriving at some sort of self-destination in the end. I collected the firewood in, enough to last three or four days. If I gathered the same amount every day, I'd have supplies of it laid up for when it rained. Hauling wet timber in wet weather in wet clothing is a sullen task to be avoided.

After stocking up with firewood, I gathered in a pile of dry bracken to lay on the floor of my tent to make a primitive but good-smelling mattress. Before actually laying it inside the tent I held the bundle in the smoke of the campfire, to drive out any insects which might be in it. Since I'd got enough meat for the evening meal, I set off without my rifle into the woods again. I mapped out the lie of the land as I went along, like memorizing the features of a street, letting my eyes and brain register various landmarks to steer by. I was careful not to step into any rabbit tracks because the smell of me would linger there and they'd find new routes to travel along. My future ninety days of survival depended upon methodical care and a form of discipline. It wasn't a Sunday morning's sport shoot I was doing, with a cooked dinner waiting for me back home whether or not I bagged the odd rabbit. It was now a case of not eating if I didn't make a kill; but that wasn't all. I had to make sure I kept myself in ultra-low key, so as not to drive the game away from my woods. I had to search out at least half a dozen separate rabbit feeding grounds, pigeon 'sitty-trees', and work them in rotation. Take rabbit or pigeon from a particular spot one day, then a different spot the next. And so on, so that by the time I came back to shoot in the first spot the small game would have settled down again.

I noted where the clumps of hazel trees grew, stuffed my pockets with ripe nuts. The trees were havens for grey squirrels, there were many dreys of them scattered around the localities of the hazel trees, within reach of Nature's larder. Squirrel meat is a tasty dish if cooked and prepared properly, and I promised myself a pot of them before the week was out. The tree rats trapezed away from me when they saw me, branch to branch, twig to twig, their tail-bushes flowing like grey-brown streamer flags. But I knew I could drop any amount I needed when I'd a mind to. Nothing difficult there. Not much meat to them as individuals, but well worth the trouble of skinning and gutting when half a dozen were in the bag. The hazel shrub trees were in heavy crop, some of the nuts ripe and others on their way to ripening. The supply seemed promisingly endless, and there were enough about for both me and the squirrels. I moved on, picking the youngest shoots of stinging nettles that I could find, filling my hat with them. Then I went back to camp.

The seemingly simple tasks had taken a long time to perform, and late afternoon was already misting in on this, my first day of aloneness. I placed my 'shopping' inside the tent, then prepared the fire. But first of all I ripped off a piece of cloth from a shirt tail and stuck the rag inside one half of the empty pellet tin I'd kept by me when I'd emptied the small bullets into the leather pouch. Waste not, want not: a cliché, but a truth. I took up a pliant piece of twig, pencil-sized, and used my jackknife spike to bore a small hole in one end. Into this hole I wedged a cigarette lighter flint until it was firmly bedded in and almost flush with the face edge of the twig. I struck another of my precious matches and set fire to the cloth inside the tin, extinguishing the flame when the cloth was well charred but still retaining plenty of 'body'. Then, by striking the twig-embedded flint with the point of my steel bowie knife I could cause a spark to jump into the tinderbox, and a gentle mouth-blowing made it glow hot enough to ignite a small sliver-paring of wood. This in turn, and with patience, got my fire going. Old Konk chuckled at me from the quiet of the glooming trees.

'That's a trick you've remembered from my telling on't, me lover. I used to make a tinderbox like that to light my fags when they put me in prison a time or two for poaching . . .'

Me too, Konk, I thought back. I did the same thing when I was in prison – was that indeed over twenty-five years ago when I was quick and lithe with youth, and the world my oyster which I soured? Time sheds its petals and its thorns, the pure and the imperfect, so quickly that there's no instant in which you can actually see the complete bloom.

They are not long, the days of wine and roses:
  Out of a misty dream
Our path emerges for a while, then closes
  Within a dream.

Not true, is it, Konk? They *are* long, the days of wine and roses. The rose is always blooming somewhere, even if unseen, and the wine of experience mellows under the cobwebs of petty irritations, brittle ambitions, broken promises. The bric-a-brac of *conscious* living.

Once I'd got the fire going with good heat at its centre core and not too much smoke billowing, I put the stinging nettles and hazelnuts into a dixie tin of water and placed the tin near the edge of heat, so that the contents would start to gather warmth, but wouldn't come to the boil until I wanted them to. I fetched the wood pigeons from the stream, removed the pebbles, and put the birds into the largest cooking tin. They looked so small and ridiculous I felt amusement, but concluded that you couldn't ridicule death when it was edible. Just cook 'em and eat 'em, then smack your lips in appreciation and maybe give a belly-burp of farewell.

Since the pigeons would take a longish time to boil into tenderness I placed the pot near to the centre of fire, covering them with plenty of water to allow for evaporation. Then I took up my rifle and went back into the darkened woods, a sliver of moon lifting its faint candleglow up to the higher stars. Birds had roosted home, rustling into comfortable perches, and ringdoves cooed good-night conversations to each other. I took up position near one of the rabbit runs I'd noted earlier on, and waited.

I seemed to wait a long time, my limbs stiffening as I crouched among the concealing bushes. I was longing to smoke my pipe, but satisfied my craving by chewing on a small cud of tobacco. The darkness deepened the woods, making it difficult to make out fine detail even through the high magnification of the telescopic sights. But I'd focused them on a fixed spot along the rabbit track, and eventually patience and planning paid off. I heard the slight noise of the rabbit before I saw it, and took up first trigger pressure. The moment the rabbit reached the spot I'd sighted on, it heading for home, I squeezed off and dropped it fair and square with a head shot.

Knowing the ways of rabbits I remained where I was, still and quiet after reloading. I sighted back onto the dead rabbit, which was still twitching in reflex death spasms. Sure enough, its mate came down the run and stopped, staring curiously at the other. Again my shot went clean to the head at about twenty-five yards' range, and I'd got two full-grown rabbits for the pot. Enough to last for two days at least. I picked them up, letting them drag and dangle on the ground so that their scent would obliterate mine and not cause other rabbits to avoid the area. Clear of the track, I took each rabbit in turn and held it by the ears in my left hand whilst I used thumb and fingers of my right to squeeze the urine from its bladder. I gutted them while they were still warm, a neat knife slit from breast to crotch, being careful not to cut into the intestines and thus contaminate the meat. Once the bellies were slit, it was simply a matter of gripping the fore-legs in one hand, the hind legs in the other, and bending the backbones across my knee to make the small bodies arch like a drawn bow, and all the guts and offal plopped out in one piece. I harled the two rabbits by cutting a slit between the tendons of one hind foot each, forcing the other foot through the slit. This made for easy carrying, like the handles of a shopping bag. Before leaving the 'pluck', the innards, I removed the hearts, liver and kidneys. These would add extra flavour to my stewpot. I left the remains for the carrion crows to feed on, or the stoats and weasels. Nature's dustbins – there was no waste in Nature, everything was recycled. Even me, one day, I thought cynically. Perhaps I'll serve as compost to strengthen the crops that the rabbits feed from.

So, back to camp to make my evening meal. I hung the harled rabbits from a nearby tree branch in safety from the night creatures, and turned my attention to the meal. The pigeons were simmering away nicely, almost ready for eating. I removed them from the dixie, placing the tin of water to one side so that the grease would congeal and serve purpose in the grease pit. I spitted the birds onto a twig and held them near the flames to crisp them up. They smelt mouth-watering good. When they were browned I dusted the flakes of fire ash from them, and the meal was ready. Three pigeons and a mush of mixed nuts and nettles. I kept the liquid from the mush to serve as a good-night drink. It was a satisfying meal that I spooned and gnawed at, even if it looked a bit messy. What the odds? – it all ended up in the same mixing bowl we call our stomachs. It was all protein, vitamins, trace elements and the like. The lack of kitchen-cupboard flavouring was fairly compensated for in the flavour of the nuts and the earthy taste of the pigeons. It was good.

When I'd finished I burned the bone debris in the fire and cleaned the dixie tins. Then, as I'd done the night before, I hunched myself in comfort round the blazing logs for a couple of hours, listening to the small winds whispering about the woods as if in search of one another. The night was fine, the patch of sky above my clearing littered with silver buttons of stars; the near shadows around me were a flickering circle of browny reds and oranges, like muted colours on an artist's palette blending in together. Beyond the tinted shadows the solid darkness stood sentinel, like a stockade giving protection to those within its walls. Lines from a poem by Robert Frost wrote themselves across my mind:

The woods are lovely, dark and deep,
But I have promises to keep,
And miles to go before I sleep.

Poor Robert, I thought. Walk on. Travel your miles. My woods are more lovely, dark and deep because no urgent promises are calling me away, no signposts are measuring out my miles. I am the contented man. I am free to sleep any time I've a mind to.

Three

The first week to ten days passed quickly enough, spiced with curry-pot seasonings of mental freshness, novelty, sweet strangeness. Enough activity to keep me physically fit and occupied, enough time to watch, or sit and let my thoughts explore any avenue they chose. Clock time was wiped away. Clock time, that hitherto heel-treading over-shoulder-breathing jailer. He was back there somewhere, treading city streets, overseeing office desks, factory conveyor belts, schools, kitchens, bus routes, church services, television programmes, this, that, and everything. Wiping his hands across everybody's life, rubbing and gnawing away like woodworm into public and private compartments of self. I felt as if I'd converted time into a cigarette end and could stub it out into an ashtray.

Time, you old Gipsy man,/Will you not stay,
Put up your caravan/Just for one day. . . ?

B'rr, b'rr, ring-ring. 'Jones speaking . . . yes, yes. I can manage a ten-minutes' interview if you get to my office ten o'clock sharp next Monday morning. Can only spare you ten minutes, I've a meeting to attend.'

'Johnny – Anna – breakfast's on the table. Hurry up, you'll be late for school else.'

'God, is that the time? I'll miss my train.'

'You're four minutes late, Miss Evans.'

'Left, right, left, right – keep in time there, you bloody

awkward squad. Keep in time, else we'll never make soldiers of you.'

'The train leaving platform five is the 11.30 for Birmingham.'

'Sorry – must dash. I'm in a hurry.'

'What time is it?'

'Anyone got the right time?'

'Drink up. We've still got time for another quick one.'

'Headquarters Control to Bandit Four. Your message timed for . . .'

Clockface time snarling itself up like a ball of wool on collision course with a bundle of kitten. Clockface time exploding into splinters and shards, and everyone trying to grab a handful in passing. Time calling the tune, directing the piper. Time scattered in bits and pieces to every horizon, like the trails of a paperchase. Wristwatches, fob watches, full and half-hunter watches, alarm clocks, grandfather and grandmother clocks, cuckoo clocks, water clocks, carriage clocks, electric and atomic clocks – even the freedom of music trapped somewhere inside the time mechanism of a metronome.

God, I thought, if only we could stand up on our hind legs and tell ourselves that we haven't got time for time. The thought amused me. I explored it.

B'rr, b'rr. 'Jones speaking. Yes, drop in when you like. What time? Time? What the hell's *time*? Just come when you feel like it.'

'Johnny – Anna – breakfast's ready when you are. The school's still standing where it usually does, if you happen to pass that way.'

'If you blokes can't keep in step, we'll never make soldiers out of you. You might as well go home.'

'The train just leaving platform five will eventually reach Birmingham.'

'Drink up. We might as well linger on and have a skinful.'

'Yes, I *know* this is a clock shop. I just don't have any time to sell.'

42

'What, the end of the world already? How time flies.'

Yes, some idiot would spoil it all by saying *that*. We used to twist our RAF motto 'way back from *'PER ARDUA AD ASTRA'* ('Through hardship to the stars') into *'PER ARDUA ASBESTOS'*, which, roughly translated, meant 'Damn you, I'm fireproof'. So, I thought, for three months I'm going to be timeproof. No food on a tray on my lap, eyes glued to the TV screen. While I'm out here in the woods, 'Crossroads' can take a running jump down 'Coronation Street', 'The Enemy at the Door' can knock as loud as it wants, and a few hundred more cowboys and Indians can litter the canyons and prairies in death postures accompanied by sad or dramatic music from a two-hundred-piece orchestra situated just out of camera sight. I remember seeing a film about a film crew making a Western film. One of the cowboy actors fired a single shot and seven pursuing Indians fell from their horses. The producer was unmoved. 'Let it go,' he said to the cameraman. 'We haven't time for a reshoot. We'll make it all fair and square by giving the film another title. We'll call it *The Magic Bullet*.'

Time, the sticky goo that clings to the feet and fingers of life. Pity we can't stick it away in some attic trunk and forget about it until it finally comes into its own and claims us in death.

On the fourth or fifth day I suddenly realized that I'd started to regard a mere water-slosh as an actual wash, and had to remedy this firmly. I dug inside myself for pride of self-discipline, and from then on took a full bath every morning in the stream, after using my lavatory pit. I'd walk naked and shivering to the water, naked except for a pair of underpants. (Strange how so-called modesty clings to us like a second skin even when there's nobody else around for maybe miles.) Once in the stream I'd slip my pants off and give them a wash while I was having one. Quite by chance – a luxury provided by Nature if ever there was one – I came upon some clumps of soapwort growing along the stream banks. By rubbing it gently with wet hands a slight lather came about, with which I could wash myself more thoroughly. After I'd washed myself and the pants, I'd wring the garment out, put them back on and return to my tent. Inside, I'd change into dry pants and hang the washed ones out to dry. I repeated this procedure every day, no matter how cold it was. To make sure that my washing was completely dry before rewearing, I'd wrap the garments around hot pebbles taken from the fire. When I'd dressed I'd drink a dixie of hot coffee, having previously roasted acorns and dandelion roots, then pounded them to gravelly lumps, then reroasted and repounded. The grit made a passable, if bitter, substitute for coffee. But the discovery of the wild soapwort really pleased me. As a boy, in my native Black Country, we called it 'foam dock', or 'wash bowl'. I gathered some of the soapwort leaves each time I washed myself at the stream, then chopped and bruised them, put them into a dixie of water and boiled them up. When cooled, the water jellified into a sort of thin soap and I used it not only for washing myself but my under-clothing and the cooking pots. There's a Yiddish saying which goes: 'God will provide – but if only He would until He does!' Not so in Nature – she'll provide everything you need if you'll take the trouble to seek it out.

During my boyhood I sometimes went fishing with Konk and some of the other men, they with their home-made fishing tackle. They'd dig at the earth with their knives in search of worm bait. If no worms were forthcoming, the men would gather in some soapwort leaves, light a small fire, and boil the leaves up in one of the empty bait tins. Then they'd stab their knives into the earth, scouring and loosening it, and pour the soapy liquid over the patch. Within seconds the worms would come bobbing to the surface, trying to get away from the soapiness which destroyed the natural slime oils around their bodies which helped them to survive and burrow underground.

When I'd drunk my sugarless and milkless coffee, I'd take up my rifle and go off in search of the next day's food supply

– I kept one step ahead, a day's step, as much as I could.

Hunting has its own strange and particular qualities. Patience and alertness are the keynotes, combined with stealth of movement and sharp ears and eyes. Take a few quiet steps, stop, listen, look. Then a few more steps. Hands and face charcoal-streaked as before, to break up the giveaway pattern of human white flesh – it's white to the quarry, no matter how tanned you may think it to be. Eyes alternately looking upwards for pigeons' 'sitty-trees', then groundwards for the spoor and droppings of rabbits. Kneel and examine the rabbit pills, eyes and experience stating whether they're old droppings or new. Rifle held steadily and firmly, pointed groundwards for safety but ready to come up to the shoulder on the instant of requirement. An air rifle is *not* a toy. One such as mine could kill a man, if the missile struck the right place. Sights zoned in at thirty yards for sureness, knowing that a degree of 'hold over' would take care of an extra ten or fifteen yards beyond that range. 'Hold over' simply means aiming at a calculated point above the one that the sights are set to. Only deep familiarity with a particular gun or rifle will ensure accuracy in using this method, but if you haven't learned this familiarity and accuracy with practice, you've no right to be shooting game. You belong on the shooting range, trying to knock holes out of pieces of white paper. A good rifle is a beautiful piece of craftsmanship from its metal parts to its wooden furniture of butt and stock. It is beautiful in form and in balance, but it doesn't have a mind. The mind and common sense remain with the shooter, so that the beauty of the rifle is after all merely an extension of his will. The rifle cannot distinguish between enemy or friend, it sends its missile to where the shooter wants it to go. And once the missile has left the muzzle, the shooter no longer has any control over it – that missile will continue to travel until some object or the force of gravity stops it. To own and use a rifle – or any weapon for that matter – is a grave responsibility.

'That's the way on it, chap,' Old Konk would mutter in my

ear. 'Always go for a sure clean kill, lad. A good clean kill – shoot only for the pot and to rid the land of pests, 'cos there's no bloody point in tekkin' life just for the sake on it . . .'

True enough. Shoot only for the pot; except when it comes to the game- and forest-keepers' natural enemies, and farmers' crop-destroying enemies like rooks, crows, magpies, jays, jackdaws, the like. None of them are really edible, so you just hang their carcases from fences or tree boughs to warn their brethren to keep away. Often, when waiting for a meal to come within reach of my rifle, I mused upon the hypocrisies which beset our society. The outcries against fox-hunting, 'nature lovers' feeding the 'pretty birds' with scraps from their dining tables, or even buying packets of peanuts for them from the supermarket. The 'Oohs' and 'Ahs' of frowning disapproval uttered up at the thought of a man lying in wait with a gun to shoot a bundle of furry love known as a rabbit.

'That's how it goes,' Konk says. 'Folks'll have a go at thee for shootin' a gun off to fill the cooking pot, then nip off to the butcher's shop for plastic-wrapped beef or mutton – they thinken meat and poultry grows ready wrapped in bloody orchards or someat.'

Stalking the woods or waiting in the bushes I let my mind do a bit of simple arithmetic. Between five and ten million pigeons in the United Kingdom – a lot of feathered fruit. A single pigeon eats up the equivalent of two loaves of bread a week, from the wheatfields, and enough malt barley a day to make around one and a quarter pints of beer. Taking the lower population of five million pigeons and allowing only a three months' crop-growing season, they get through enough stuff to make over 100 million loaves of bread every year, and over 550 million pints of beer. Add to this the fact that they fly off with an annual multi-tonnage of clover, peas, rape, seed grass, brussels sprouts, broccoli, winter cabbage, beans – amounting to at least £50 million pounds' worth – no wonder farmers and keepers reach for their twelve-bores when they hear them cooing their love songs to each other.

I had to creep up on the birds while they were on the ground or perched in their 'sitty-trees', then take long and careful aim. The shot had to be angled exactly right because a pigeon, like a crow, has a fine defence mechanism built into the grain of its feathers. When the feathers are closed up tight they can deflect even the high-powered pellets from a twelve-bore shotgun. But I can honestly say that in the whole three months of my aloneness I shot nothing except by a clean kill, with one exception. If I had any doubts about range, windage or anything else, I just didn't shoot. With pigeons, my system was to shoot a couple or three while they were easy targets and then use them as decoys, setting them up in the flight paths of other pigeons so they shouldn't be off seeing them. I'd place the decoys in an open patch of land, but within rifle shot. I staked the decoys by placing a small Y-shaped twig under the neck of each to keep the birds' heads erect, making sure they were facing into the wind. Pigeons, like most birds, feed into the wind so's not to get their feathers ruffled. I'd spread the wings slightly to show the black and white markings, since I belong to the school of thought which believes that it is these markings which tell pigeons in flight that it's safe to land and eat. Six to eight pigeons was all that I'd take at one shoot, enough to fill my stomach for a couple of days, since, other than the stream, I had no way of keeping them fresh. I've never had the palate for high game, even pheasant and hare, which is left to hang until the flesh turns almost green and smells like a sewer.

The exception to my clean kills was the day I came up against a buck hare. I stalked in to him against the wind to keep my smell from him, seeing him flattened on a mound of earth with ears erect and twitching, eyes rolling to give him all-round vision. I got inside twenty yards of him, but he didn't present me with a clear head shot. I sighted carefully three inches above the portion of head I could see, took up first trigger pressure and centred the crosshairs of the 'scope on the chosen spot. Then I clucked my tongue, making a short sharp sound. The hare's head came up quickly, on full alert. I squeezed off the shot. But even so, my quarry moved at the last instant and the missile took him in the shoulder instead of the head. Startled, frightened, he scudded away, ears flattened along the length of his body to streamline his race against pain. He ran straight, not zig-zagging as chased hares usually do. My first frantic impulse was to go after him, put him out of his misery – but I knew I mustn't do this. If I went after him he'd keep running, his adrenalin working overtime to put distance between us. He'd outrun me, even with the wound, and I'd never find him. He would hole up some place and die slowly, maybe taking days; growing weaker and weaker until stoat, weasel or fox smelled him out. Or, if they didn't get him, gangrene would.

I forced myself to light my pipe and wait for twenty minutes or so, knowing that once he realized he wasn't being chased the hare would find a hiding place to rest and lick his wound. Then he'd stiffen up and be unable to run. I waited my good twenty minutes, then picked up his blood spoor with my eyes and went after him. I found him motionless but alive in a thicket, hiding in the brambles. A final shot, and he was finished. But I cursed myself for having fouled up on my first shot, causing the creature unnecessary suffering.

I gutted and harled the hare in the usual way, leaving the entrails for predators, and went back to camp with it. I stopped along the way to gather a crop of field mushrooms. I hesitated about them at first, wondering if they *were* mushrooms. They might have been toadstools. But Old Konk ghost-spoke inside me.

'Cull thee memory, boy. Trust thee memory to tell thee the truth on't. Small white caps . . . short stems . . . dark brown gills, lack of nasty smell. Bisn't they mushrooms, then?'

I decided they were mushrooms all right, gathered them in.

The woods and stream banks were rich with wild parsnip, dandelion leaves, sow thistle, chickweed, nettles, nuts and acorns. I was living well off them, and the only thing I seemed to lack was a little salt flavouring. I collected large bunches of mixed leaves and plants. Meadowsweet, colts-foot, some bearberry and heather. Some of the bunches I hung inside my tent to dry naturally, other bunches I set round the fire to dry artificially. The leaves were past their best at this time of year, but they'd suffice when finger-shredded and mixed. My pipe tobacco was giving out and I wasn't giving up.

The blackberries had come to full ripeness, I noted, and I'd pick some next day. They'd make a nice sweet dish mixed with chopped hazelnuts, and some I could crush and mix with water to make a cordial to sip at, hot or cold.

I unloaded my wares at the campsite, hung the harled hare from the usual tree branch, then filled my water containers at the stream. I could see fair-sized fish darting and silvering in and out of the reeds but I couldn't identify them. I'd never been much of a fisherman – as long as the fish filled the pan and stomach I never gave much heed to the species. These could have been perch, roach, rudd, dace – those were just names. You can't cook and eat a name. The things swishing and swirling in the water were *fish*, that's all that mattered . . .

I sat on the bank to figure out ways to catch some . . . sitting so there was a sort of time-slip and my mind bridged the years to when I was a boy of twelve years or so, before the war, and I was with my Dad and Old Konk. Konk seemed old even then. I think he was born old. He'd turned up that long-ago day carrying a mysterious parcel; he'd come into the back kitchen of our house in the Black Country (just under thirty miles from where I was now sitting on the stream bank), stepping carefully onto the bleached sacks which covered the floor quarries, as if the sacks were carpets in a mansion.

'Just paying a social call, me lovers,' he wheezed. 'Just thought I'd drop in for a cup of tea, like.'

'It'll have to be breadcrumb tea,' Dad answered. 'With

condensed milk. We'n got none of the proper sort, nor any dole money left to buy any with.'

'As long as it's wet and warm,' Konk said.

We watched Dad make the breadcrumb tea. He sprinkled breadcrumbs onto the hot fire hob and when they were burned this side of black he scooped them onto a platter and ground them into powder with a knife handle. He put a spoonful into each cup, poured in boiling water from the kettle steaming on its trivet, then added half a spoonful of condensed milk for sweetness and colouring. We sipped and slurped at it.

'There's no work about,' Old Konk said. 'Just no work.'

'I know it,' Dad answered grimly. 'I thought of going for a sojer. They want men in Spain to stop Franco's lot.'

'A lot of men from hereabouts bist going. Me, I had enough sojering in Flanders and on the Somme.'

'The government's trying to stop the men joining up,' Dad mused, 'but they'm going just the same. They can send money home.'

'Until they'm killed,' Konk grimaced. 'The money stops, then. There's many a house wi' drawn curtains. Many a woman sitting by a cold hearthstone wi' her apron over her head so's the kids won't see her crying.'

'What'n you got there?' Dad inquired, as Konk started to unwrap the parcel. The newspaper wrappings fell away and he displayed a boy's dream of a model sailing ship. A galleon, two feet long, with white calico sails, and rigging made from waxed string. I felt envy for it as big as my mind. I wanted to shrink my size and walk its quarterdeck with a cutlass and pistols strapped to my belt, giving orders to the first mate to lay on hard with the cat-o'-nine-tails. In a split second of seeing the boat I was already its captain, and I'd got the second mate – whom I didn't like for some reason I forget – strapped to the main mast undergoing punishment before the assembled crew. Once the flogging was over, I was going to make the second mate walk the plank, and then keelhaul him before casting him adrift in an open boat. Probably the

50

second mate reminded me of our headmaster at school.

'It's a beauty,' Dad said, eyeing it from every angle, 'a real beauty. Where'd it come from, Konk?'

'I made it,' Konk replied modestly. 'I'm not just a rogue and a vagabond, thee knows. I'n got talent as well. I copied it from an old picture.' He looked at me.

'It's for thee, me lover,' he said. My heart almost stopped beating. 'Only thee hast to let thee Dad and me have a play wi' it as well,' he continued, eyes twinkling, 'now and again.'

He looked at Dad. Some sort of message passed between them. Dad's mouth crinkled to a grin.

'We might as well give it a try straightaway,' he murmured.

'Ar, we might as well,' Konk agreed.

We all three walked to a copse two miles or so away, where lay private land with a huge lake stocked with fish.

'It's a trout farm,' Konk told me, 'so we have to walk a bit on the sly side, 'cos we bist trespassing. We'm breaking the law, and the law don't like being broken. Very sensitive, is the law.'

'So's my belly,' Dad muttered, 'but it'll feel all the better for a bit of trout rubbed into its insides.'

Our spirits had revived as we left the dark, sombre shapes of glassworks and iron foundries behind, got clear of the slum streets of back-to-back houses, the gloom of idle pit heads and the dusty grey slate quarries which waited for men to come back again and tremble their masses with charge blastings. We were in open country now, heading towards Shropshire's border, and the hedges were busy entertaining bees and scents, and grasshoppers plucking at the breeze like muted violin strings. Up ahead, in the far distance, we could see the crest of Shropshire's Wrekin hill, mist round its head like a scarf; behind us, diminished by space and haze, we could just make out the Clent hills of Worcestershire . . . the past and present merged . . . I was so physically near to that spot we'd 'visited' all those years ago I could have reached it in half an hour by car . . .

'Come on, young 'un,' Konk said to me, 'and carry the boat with thee.'

We picked our ways through bracken and trees, and there in front of us was the lake. Konk's and Dad's eyes were real greedy.

'Pass the boat,' Konk said, and I watched as he fixed eyelet screws to the underneath of the keel. From the screws he hung lengths of fishing line, and on the end of these strands he fixed hooks.

'Now for the bait,' he muttered, and took a tin from his pocket which, when he opened it, showed a mass of maggots inside. He fixed a bait maggot to each hook – eight in all – and gave me back the boat and a ball of string.

'Go and play with thee boat, me lover,' he told me, 'while me and your Dad has a nice lie down on the grass just out of sight. Now set the sails so's the boat crosses from here to there, the other side. See? Keep the boat tied to the string so's thee don't lose it. Play it in and out like a fishing line, and if any keeper comes up on you, just act all innocent and say you'm playing with your boat and knows nothing about the laws o' trespass. Get it?'

I got it. That lake was alive with fish. I played the boat from one shore to another and when it crossed to Konk's side he or my Dad would lift it out of the water, unhook the fish dangling there, rebait the hooks and replay the boat back to me. Inside two hours we'd caught more fish than a dozen Irish navvies could eat after a Saturday night's booze-up. Finally Konk signalled me to put a halt to it, and join him and Dad. We carried the fish off in sacks Dad and Konk unfurled from their pockets. They carried the sacks, I carried the boat, hugging the precious vessel to me tight as a secret. Tagging behind the men, I was once more the captain of the galleon giving the headmaster–second mate a good whipping with the cat-o'-nine-tails wielded by the first mate.

The present dropped like a pebble into the memories of the past, spreading ripples of now-ness into my thoughts. I still hadn't come up with any ideas of how to catch fish from the stream. Could I dam the water and catch them that way? No. It would take too long and in any case, even if I succeeded, I'd like as not upset the landowner by whose courtesy I was occupying the woods. I recalled that the gamekeeper, Mr Turner, had told me on the day of my arrival that he'd leave some rabbit-trapping wire for me in his hidey-hole hut – perhaps I could collect it tomorrow and fashion some fishing hooks. I could dig worms for bait, and maybe use strong briars for lines. It was worth a try – and there were a couple of safety pins holding the zip fastener of my sleeping bag together . . . fresh fish would make a change in my diet of pigeon, squirrel and rabbit meat.

Before cooking my evening meal, and there being enough daylight still to see by, I went out and shot a couple of crows and a jackdaw. These would serve to nail to Mr Turner's hut door as promised, in part payment for the trapping wire.

I sat down to my late meal eventually: mushrooms, chickweed and the remains of a rabbit from yesterday. Tomorrow, I'd parboil the freshly caught hare, then fire-roast it.

After eating, as was my now every evening habit, I sat and smoked my pipe by the friendly campfire until it was time to turn in. I felt, in some strange comforting way, that Old Konk sat opposite me with ferret-twitching pockets and eyes a-twinkle, puffing his clay pipe and planning his next poaching expedition.

Four

Late September still had the taste of August in its mouth, as if it had drunk in the smells of harvesting and the smells lingered on its breath. The morning and evening air had a chill to it, and winter's advance banners of mist. But for the most part the weather was good between dawn and dusk, and life with it was good too. Slow-paced and unhurried, attuned to the harmonies of Nature. A world populated by me alone, it seemed, and birds and small beasts.

The starlings had reached the halfway house between youth and adulthood, their bodies almost fully grown but their heads still chicklike. They kept together in flocks, communal living, and wouldn't pair off for mating for their first year. They thrived on the blackberry fruits, and a time or two I shot enough to provide a meal. A dozen of the young birds, seasoned with various wild herbs and supplemented with plant food, made a good meal. The swifts had already departed for warmer climates, seeking the stronger sunlight, and now the swallows were patchworking the skies like clouds of soot dust chased by the wind. They too would soon be gone, making for Africa to bask in a new summer. They'd worn out the English one.

The man-given names of the various woodland plants and shrubs ever pleased me, because they sounded like music running through clear water, names from a poet's imagery store. Traveller's joy with its white feathered seeds which would light the way into spring, parasol mushrooms to keep the rain off the tiny scurrying insects, meadow saffron pushing cream-mauve buds through the earth; red leg, lady's mantle; 'kisses' or 'gipsy comb' (burdock); 'maid-of-the-meadow' or 'goat's-beard' for meadowsweet, 'joy of the mountains' for marjoram; 'shepherds' clock' for wild thyme . . . lime, broom, heather, knapweed, lords and ladies, star of Bethlehem, silverweed, jewel weed, chickweed, sweet gale, cloudberry . . . the names go on and on, hemmed in only by the boundaries of imagination. Lovely, lovely names, sweet sounding. Names handed down from generation to generation, sometimes getting a bit altered in the telling, but keeping the fragrance yet. I remember, once, writing a story and wanting to disguise the location which I wrote about. In reality the story was written around a region called 'The Clock Fields' and I altered this to read 'The Dandy Fields'. Long after publication of the story, I learned that a couple of hundred years ago the region *had* been known as 'The Dandy Fields'. I suppose, originally, they'd been called 'The Dandy Clock Fields', when children blew away the parachute-like seeds from the dandelions to 'tell the time'. The 'Dandy' got lopped off in the telling. But, in the names of the plants and the trees, the fields and the spinneys, old memories still linger, old ghosts still whisper happily together from the buds of springtime to the blazing falling leaves of autumn. The fields and spinneys, trees and shrubs, streams and buries, birds and beasts, bridlepaths, sky and wind and earth still hold and carry the pollen of memories of men like Konk . . . and I hope one day, men like me. A poem written under the name of 'E.R.' sums up Old Konk in better words than I can coin:

He had the ploughman's strength
In the grasp of his hand.
He could see a crow
Three miles away,
And the trout beneath the stone.
He could hear the green oats growing,
And the sou'-west making rain;

And the wheel upon the hill
When it left the level road.
He could make a gate, and dig a pit,
And plough as straight as stone can fall.
And he is dead.

No, not dead. Just gone away. I'd find him somewhere threading a ferret from a line, or sprawled upon a grassy bank, waiting for my Dad to come up so they could moach off together and let their eyes and ears tell them where the game was. String in my Dad's boot eyelets instead of laces; women back there in the cramped streets with bellies plump through childbearing and not food. Hungry days . . . hard days . . . poachers days . . .

'What's that you've got in that sack, Dad?'

'Nothing.'

'It's squiggling about, isn't it?'

'Ar, it's a lot of nothing just having a squiggle about. When you puts a lot of nothing in a sack together, it don't half squiggle.'

And off he'd go with his ferrets. Back he'd come with the rabbits. A lot of nothing seemed to gather interest the more there was of it.

But at least the poaching man of my boyhood seemed to have an instinctive intimacy with Nature, recognizing that he is part of her, and not her overlord. I've no doubt in my mind that some of the olden-time poachers helped to christen a few of the wild plants. 'Wortcunning' is a name given to a wild plant having medicinal properties. I can recall snatches of conversation between Black Country men who used words and expressions handed down to them from generations of ancestors.

'How'd you manage to slip past the gamekeepers wi' that lot, Will?'

'Ah managed. Ah wert cunning about it.'

Wortcunning. 'Wert cunning'. Ah, well.

* * *

57

I walked across the fields to Mr Turner's hidey-hut, carrying the dead carrion birds that I'd shot with me. A bumblebee seemed to lead the way, droning in front of me, its fat body seeming too large to be supported, let alone airborne, by its short gossamer wings. It droned like an old man basking in sleep and sunlight in a deck chair. Bumblebee – humblebee is its real English name, being considered of less importance by our forebears than the richness-giving honey bee. Yet, following in the lazy wake of the creature, I felt that I liked the name bumblebee better, because that's what it seemed to do. Bumble along, a small lollipop on wings, ready to go where the breeze took it. The tumbleweed bumblebee, as English as England. Off he went, poaching his pollen wherever he could find it – as it should be, I thought. A happy poacher is more self-fulfilled than a bored gamekeeper.

I approached the hidey-hut with stealth, not because I intended to steal anything but because I wanted to veer off if Mr Turner or anyone else was around. I wanted to honour my three months' contract with aloneness. No human company was the rule I had to steer by.

But I needn't have been so cautious, because the hut and its site were deserted. I pushed inside the creaking door, the sunlight peering over my shoulder to give me light to see by. The shed was small but tidy, with a small storm lanthorn hanging from the rafters. There was a home-made armchair, assembled from logs and the seat padded with cured rabbit skins. A small window in each wall enabled the occupant to see out on all sides, to see what was going on in the surrounding fields and woodlands. On the walls, hanging from hooks, nails, or on made-from-log shelves was an assortment of useful bits and pieces. String, wire, saws, log-splitting chisels, nets, gate hinges and jars of screws. It all looked like a small village ironmonger's shop.

I poked around with curiosity, pausing now and then to examine an article more thoroughly. A couple of well-oiled gin traps were hanging from a wooden peg, and next to them an old man-trap. When set, the wicked teeth of the trap would clamp round the legs of a man and hold him fast and painfully until the keepers of bailiwicks could get to him and take him into custody. Illegal for over a hundred years now, the man trap was obviously just a keepsake of Mr Turner's.

I was amazed at one find hanging over the shed doorway: a flintlock musket. I took it down and examined it, feeling excitement well up inside me as I eventually recognized it for what it was – a 'Brown Bess' rifled musket, used by British infantry in the Napoleonic wars. It was in beautiful condition. Designed around 1730, the Brown Bess was to remain in service for almost a hundred years. No one seems to know where the word 'Brown' comes from, unless it be because of the walnut wood furniture, but 'Bess' is most like derived from the German *Büchse*, meaning 'gun'. Originally the weapon fired a ball three-quarters of an inch in diameter, a deadly missile. Big enough to stop an elephant, let alone Napoleon's army. I thought the piece to be quite valuable, a collector's item, and wondered why Mr Turner should be so careless or uncaring as to leave it here in his hidey-hut where any stray gipsy or poacher could chance upon it and bear it away. I could only conclude that Mr Turner liked to cling to remnants of the distant past, and chanced keeping the rifle here so that it gave him a sense of contentment when he sat here to 'study the moods of the fields and woods' as he'd put it. Reluctantly, I replaced the gun above the door, feeling my fingers stick to it like greed itself.

As promised, he'd left some trapping wire for me. Next to it he'd laid out some short nails and a tacking hammer. I tacked the dead birds to the outside of his shed where he couldn't be off seeing them, and took the trapping wire away with me. I'd seen some busy-looking rabbit runs and droppings on my way over from the wood where the campsite was, and figured on taking a few. I'd got half a dozen prepreared hazelmast stakes with me, already sharpened at one end with my bowie knife. The stakes were about eighteen inches long and three inches in circumference. I fixed the trapping-wire lengths to the stakes as I walked along, making nooses which

59

I fixed firmly to the unpointed ends of the staves. I laid the traps at irregular intervals along the runs, driving the pointed ends well into the ground, so that the nooses stood some eight or nine inches high. They had to be placed in such a position that the rabbits I intended to catch would be in a forward hop when their heads entered the nooses, and the vermin's own weight would cause the noose to run tight and garrot it. As I set each trap I rubbed it over with a piece of rabbit pelt I carried, to remove my human smell, then disguised it as much as possible with grass. Six traps set, and with luck when I came back that evening at least one would be holding a dead rabbit for me.

For the past couple of days I'd felt an urge to do some writing, but I hadn't got pen or paper to scribble away with. So, once more I knocked at Mother Nature's cupboard door. She let me poke about inside, allowing me to have memory as a chair to stand on. Off I went into the woods to search for inkhorns, members of the toadstool family commonly known as ink-caps, academically as *Coprinus*. They take their name of ink-caps from olden times, because they resemble the medieval inkwells made from ramshorn used by the then monks and scholars. I found some clusters of the fungi whose gills had darkened and the cap flesh had started to dissolve. I picked them carefully so's not to burst them, put them into a dixie tin and placed the tin near the heat of the fire. This speeded up the spore discharge and caused the ink-caps to melt into a black thickish liquid, which gave me the writing ink I needed. Now for pen and paper, I thought. The pen was easily arrived at, since I had plenty of pigeon feathers to choose from, to make quills. I could make paper from tree bark, and while searching for a suitable sort could collect some oak-marble galls. These, formed by the larvae of gall wasps, could be boiled to extract the rich tannic acid which in turn could be mixed in with the ink-cap fluid to make it more fast and permanent. In olden times, way back with the Ancient Greeks and Egyptians, paper was known as papyrus and was made by glueing strips of bulrush pith together.

60

Well, I didn't actually require papyrus as such, only something to write on. I settled for the bark of birch trees. Birch has a remarkable resistance towards wet, damp and decay. I chose the bark carefully, cutting it from birch tree branches where the loss wouldn't be injurious to the tree itself. Even so, I didn't cut the bark in complete circles round the limbs, but took patches which would eventually heal over. I had to dry the patches carefully by the campfire. Too much heat would make the fragments brittle and powdery. A slow-heat drying prevented this, leaving the inside skin of the bark just about suitable for writing on with the Nature-provided ink and the pigeon-provided pen. Not exactly a brilliantly laid out printing press, but there again, even Caxton had to start somewhere. I could at least now jot down thoughts which I wanted to preserve, and thus hold a more solid form of communication at least with myself.

Only once was I clouded over inside with a feeling of loneliness which almost bordered upon depression. I'd got a desire to talk with friends, listen to music or a radio broadcast, or visit a pub and swap yarns with old men in corners. The alarm clock of birds woke me as usual but I lay in my sleeping bag wondering what the devil I was doing here, over half a century old, playing Last of the Mohicans. There was a deep mist outside, giving way to a drizzle of rain. Just a feathering of rain, but it added to my depressed feelings. It had been raining on and off for three days now, and I'd used up my reserve food store. I lay in the tent listening to the wood noises. A pigeon low-roared a complaint somewhere; a crow rasped his voice across the air as rough as emery paper. The dead leaves around the tent seemed to come alive and whisper amongst themselves as breaths of wind snagged against them. The wet smell, the damp smell of woods, seemed suddenly oppressive and all-confining. Smell of earth, like new-dug graves in a churchyard. Only bird chirps, miserable as misery, and rustling leaf noises existed to lean against the heavy silence. The small sounds were no more than mice feet scampering across my awareness. I felt alone and abandoned, self-pitying. I scrabbled reluctantly from my bed, made use of the toilet pit, then forced myself to the stream to take the morning plunge. Shivering and miserable, I then got dressed, took up my rifle and went in search of food. I scoured the woods and bordering fields for small game, but none was about. The squirrels and pigeons were sheltering out of sight. I almost decided to give up, go back to camp and climb into my bed and doze the day away. There was just enough squirrel and herb stew to serve me frugally.

Then one of the distant fields with its herd of wet huddled cows struck a chord in my memory and I almost laughed aloud as I realized I'd got a deep craving – for salt. My mouth watered at the thought of it. I'd had no direct salt in my system for a long time, and it was crying out for some. I entered the fields and searched along the barbed-wired perimeter until I found what I was looking for, a huge rock-like cow lick of brownish salt, placed there by the herdsman for the cattle to rub their tongues on. I broke a goodish chunk off and headed urgently back to camp with it. It took me a long time in the dampness, but at last I got the fire burning with the aid of twigs from the grease pit. I placed the dixie of squirrel and herb stew over the flames after adding generous quantities of the newly acquired salt, and when it was all warmed up I wolfed it down. It tasted better than a brew of good ale on a hot day. Even as I ate the food the rain drizzle petered out, the autumn sun shone through the clouds in a warm smile that embraced me and everything, and the vanishing mist danced strange patterns through the vague-shaped trees. I immediately felt better and more cheerful, glad to be alive, glad to be glad.

I went to the stream and checked the fishing lines I'd put out the night before. A mixture of bent safety pins and wire, with lines made from thin, strong briars. The bait had been taken from the hooks, but there were no fish. I philosophically rebaited, checked the firmness of the tether sticks which kept the lines anchored to the bank, then set off into the woods again. I built the fire up first with good thick logs and placed my damp washing round it at a safe distance. Sun and fire would soon dry it out.

Whilst checking the fishing lines I'd heard pheasants coughing deep in the woods, and decided to go after a brace. Turner, the gamekeeper, had told me when I arrived that he didn't mind me taking the odd bird or two. Anyway, the main shoot was over and done with. It hadn't interfered with me in any way, the reports of the twenty or so shotguns being muffled by distance. In fact, the pheasant shoot had done me something of a favour, sending more small game and birds into my own woods where no heavy guns raged, and there was safety by comparison. I'd watched the shoot through the 'scope of my own gun, and somehow felt that there was no sport to it at all. Rearing the chick pheasants by hand so that they became half-tame in their adulthood, then banging away at 'em with barrels of ball shrapnel seemed a bit lopsided to me. A twelve-bore shotgun makes a large pattern-spread of buckshot, and I couldn't see how anyone could miss if the target were within range. Just point and fire and then retrieve, it seemed to me.

I like to know that I can put a candleflame out at thirty yards with a single shot, four times out of six minimum, and know I'm on top form. I'd been a marksman with the RAF police years ago, and was crack shot with rifle or pistol. There's a great deal of difference between the use of each weapon. You *aim* a rifle but you *point* a pistol. With a rifle you close one eye to line up the rear and foresight; shooting a pistol, you keep both eyes open and make the weapon an extension of your hands. During the Palestine war of 1946–48 we learned the best way to shoot a pistol was the method which came to be known as 'the Palestine Crouch'. This meant using both hands to the pistol, crouching the body so that arms and elbows covered the chest and heart regions. One hand gripped the butt of the pistol while the other hand supported the firing hand with palm placed under the butt itself. This gave for more accurate shooting.

When I see television newsreels or cops-and-robbers action films today, I see that this stance is invariably used. The modern shootist seems to have learned from us.

I remember how my reputation as a pistol-shooter once soared higher than a bullet, so that I was constantly challenged on the practice range by officers and men alike. We'd just returned from a desert horse patrol to stables, two of us, early one morning. We'd put our horses into the stable lines and were walking back to our billets for a shower, breakfast and bed. At one end of the stable yard, a good thirty yards away, was an adobe wall with a Coca-Cola bottle left on it by one of the Arab syces. Thirty yards is one hell of a range for an accurate pistol shot, it being more of a close-quarters weapon. My patrol partner – a compulsive gambler if there ever was one – threw down the gauntlet. 'One dinar,' he said (a dinar being the equivalent to the late English pound). 'One shot each. Nearest to the bottle wins the bet.' We tossed a coin to decide who'd take first shot, and it fell in my favour.

Apart from the stance taken to fire a pistol – a revolver, that is – there are two ways of firing one, since it has double action. You can squeeze the trigger direct, which means that the hammer will rise and fall onto the cartridge in one movement, or you can cock the hammer and then fire. The latter method, although a fraction slower in action, lightens the pressure needed to activate the trigger, thus eliminating barrel wobble. I favour this method myself, and did so at the time of the bet. As I drew my pistol from my hip holster my thumb was already drawing the hammer back to full-cock position. I wasn't looking at the bottle, I was looking down at the pistol. I was still looking at it when it cracked off its shot and smashed the bottle into fragments.

Nobody could have been more surprised than me: it was a fluke shot. My thumb hadn't quite brought the hammer ratchet to its fixed position and it slipped from my thumb and detonated the cartridge. But I didn't bat an eyelid. I just blew the wisp of cordite smoke from the muzzle, cowboy fashion, ejected the empty and reloaded with a live round before returning the weapon to holster. My companion stared at me with awe and amazement.

'Shooting's one thing,' he said, 'but that was *shooting*.' As I pocketed my winnings, I hadn't got the heart to tell him it was a sheer accident. I remembered another shoot up in Norfolk, a pheasant shoot. I was friendly with the gamekeeper whose bailiwick it was. When the gentry came in with their matched pairs of twelve-bores I helped out as beater until they'd bagged their fill. A couple of days after the main shoot was over it was customary for the landowner to let his tenant farmers clean up the crumbs, as it were. It was like a scene from the Keystone Cops gunning for the Dead-End Kids, the Dead-End Kids being the bewildered pheasants. By the time the tenant farmers turned up, some partly drunk and others completely so, at mid afternoon, I felt a body would be safer back on the Normandy invasion beaches.

One old gaffer of a farmer actually had the barrel of his single-shot gun bound up in layers of copper wire, bunched strands of it, where the metal had bulged through age and overfiring. The gamekeeper had difficulty in getting them to take up their positions and hold there, so they wouldn't cross one another's guns. The sharp air was rich with whisky and brandy fumes. Yet another farmer was using a black-powder muzzle-loading gun which he claimed to have used from boyhood and which was an inheritance from his grandfather. He claimed it was the best gun in the country, and tried to slur his way through an account of how he'd captured a suspected German parachutist with it while serving with the Home Guard. Another farmer shouted him down, crying out that 'it weren't no bleddy German, it were a bleddy motorcyclist wearing a bleddy leather hat and goggles who'd lost his way in the blackout.' The owner of the muzzle-loader kept dropping the tiny fulminate caps which fitted over the firing nipples of the piece, until he eventually lost the lot so couldn't do any shooting. Being a sportsman he volunteered to act as beater and staggered off into the copse making enough noise to raise the dead from Custer's Last Stand, let alone the pheasants. He was sing-roaring something which sounded vaguely as if it were his delight on a Sat'dy night in the seaz'n of the year – interjected with a muffled curse or two as the brambles and briars tried to fight him to a stand-still.

Another farmer was using a double-barrelled .410 gun – far too light for the job in hand, but he wasn't going to bag anything anyway. I watched in astonishment curled up inside a grin as he blearily and beerily tried to load one of the barrels with a tube of Polo mints. He'd got the sweets mixed up with the loose cartridges in his pocket, and Polo mints and cartridges were about the same diameter size; except that there was no rim to the mint tube packet and every time he inserted it into the breech of his gun it slid along the barrel and plopped onto the ground. He kept picking it up owlishly and re-inserting it. From time to time he'd take a sip from a hip flask of brandy, then try loading up again.

'Are we going to beat for *that* lot?' I asked aghast.

'We're going to beat it all right,' my gamekeeper friend replied, 'in that direction, as fast as our heels can carry us. We're going to give this bloody lot a bit of leg-bail.' He pointed to the rearwards of the farmers, and that's the direction we took off in. Nobody ever gave faster 'leg-bail' to a scene than we did, leg-bail meaning to run away.

In a good season the population of pheasants throughout the country can reach as high as the twenty million mark, about half the number being wild and the other half hand-reared and finally released for the gun syndicates to play cowboys and Indians with. Out of the twenty million I only wanted a couple, just to vary my diet a bit. From darkness to dawn they'd keep to their tree perches, and these were the best hours for a poacher to be abroad. Not only for secrecy's sake, but for the ease of 'bagging'. A casual walk through a pheasant copse or spinney during daylight hours, without incriminating guns or trapping instruments, would spell out the lie of the land to the expert eye. Eyes to the ground, not up to the trees. Pheasants roosted several to a bough, always facing against the wind so's their feathers remained unruffled. Keen eyes could pick out the bird droppings on the ground, and then it was a simple matter to mark that place and come back to it at night with a gun. The art was never to shoot at one bird frontways on, but to sight up sideways. Then a single shot could drop several birds at once.

As I went in search of my pheasants I had no need of the stealth necessary for poacher against gamekeeper, only the stealth to bring me within range of the ground-feeding targets. But even as I crept through the woods of the present, part of my mind still lingered in copses of the past . . . there was Dad and Old Konk on private land with not a gun between them, trying to catch pheasants by moonlight. They'd got nets, a wire strangle noose apiece on long poles – the idea being to lower the nooses gently over the roosting birds' heads then jerk them down from their perches – and they'd got bird lime. Bird lime was a black sticky tarlike substance which, when smeared on a tree perch, caught the birds fast by the claws. This night in particular they'd smeared several perches with bird lime, and they caught a parrot. I was acting as lookout for the two men when I heard this hell of a commotion coming from among the bushes, squawkings and screechings and flapping of wings mixed in with Dad's curses and Konk's braying hysterical chuckles.

'Grab the bloody thing and quieten it,' I heard Dad whisper in a voice that could be heard three fields away.

'Thee do it,' Konk gurgled. 'It seems to have tekken a liking to thee.'

'Get the bloody thing off'n my back. It's claws bist stuck in my jacket.'

'Shouldn't wear thee best jacket when thee teks a walk by moonlight.'

'Silly bugger – it's the only jacket I've got.'

Between them they disentangled the raving parrot, and Dad clamped a hand round its beak to keep it quiet.

'What'll we do wi' it, Konk?'

'I dunno. Can we eat it? Looks big as an ostrich to me.'

'Don't think we can eat it. Never heard o' anybody eating a parrot.'

'Best kick it up the arse and sent it back to Africky, then.'

'I don't really want it,' Dad said generously. 'I know we usually goes halves wi' everything we catchen, but you can have all of this 'un.'

'No, I couldn't rob thee of it, me lover. You can keep all of it for theeself.'

'I don't bloody well *want* it.'

'Nor me. I already got me a parrot at home, only it calls itself me wife.'

I could see them there in the moonlight, the parrot now perched on Dad's shoulder, him looking like Long John Silver in *Treasure Island*. I started to laugh.

'Shurrup,' Dad bellowed at me, 'else we'll have every copper and keeper in the district down on us.'

He and Konk eventually sold the parrot to a publican for a poundnote so they felt they'd put a good night's work in despite the fact they caught no pheasants. I got a penn'orth of gobsuckers out of the deal, so didn't do so badly either. We never did find out from whose zoo or aviary the parrot had escaped. I don't suppose the parrot particularly cared either.

Up ahead of me, in a corner of a field near the tree line, I could see several brown heads bobbing up and down as beaks stabbed insects from the ground. A cluster of hen pheasants, with one more brightly plumed cock amongst them. I inched nearer and nearer until the range was down to fifteen yards. They hadn't spotted or heard me. This seemed to be a common weakness amongst pheasants which had survived a big shoot. Their reflexes seemed to slow down, like shellshock victims, and it took some time for them to recover their usual alertness. I'd once seen a pheasant lie down as if shot when a car backfired shortly after the guns had been at work.

I decided to take the cock first, and hoped to make a quick reload and get one of the hens on the rebound of surprise. I aimed, squeezed off, and the cock stood motionless. Not a flutter or a twitter came from him, but I knew that he was dead; he just died upright and stayed locked in that position. The hens stopped feeding, looked around them with darting, almost snakelike, heads because they sensed that something was amiss. I remained quiet and still until they set to feeding again, then softly reloaded and took one of the hens. The others didn't take to the air, they just ran away with necks outstretched and bodies hugging the ground as they ran. I aimed six inches in front of a hen running at right-angles to me, and she toppled over as she and the slug met. The others disappeared into the scrub, but I was satisfied with my catch and collected them in. The birds were ripe and plump, enough for three good meals. I'd got some wild parsnip roots which I could slice into chips, and enough grease to cook them in. Pheasant and chips for supper. I made a beano of a feast.

I parboiled one of the pheasants after I'd plucked and gutted it, then took it from the salted water and threaded a stick through it and balanced the stick over the hottest embers of fire by way of a trivet I'd rigged up, supported by two other sticks with 'Y' ends. Every now and again I turned the bird on the trivet so that the flesh slowly roasted and crisped up. Whilst it was roasting I fried up the parsnip chips with some steaks of fungi puff ball. The fungus was firm and fresh, not having approached anywhere near to its bursting stage when the skin would be swollen with pepper-like powder, waiting for the winds to burst it and spread its cloud of khaki-coloured pollen seeds.

You can keep your parrots, Konk, I thought. They might look pretty enough in a cage or on Dad's shoulder, but you can't beat a nicely cooked pheasant and Nature's trimmings lining the inside of your belly. And stars for company, and spitting sparks from the fire logs.

'That's the way on't,' Konk ghost-voiced back. 'Feather, fin or fur – it's all there for the tekkin' of it. Eat well, me lover, and keep thee self in good fettle.'

Goodnight, Konk.

Goo'night, me lover.

Five

The period of my aloneness wasn't all taken up with mere survival. There was a lot of time for thought and self-analysis. I'd got fungi ink, pigeon-feather quills and bark parchment to write on when I'd a mind to. It was mostly a form of poetry I wrote, because I wanted to make capsules of my thoughts and impressions, condense them into an essence which I could add to later on if I wanted to. Besides which, in writing, I'm of the opinion that poetry calls for the greatest discipline. The end product has to have, for the reader, the taste of clear simplicity combined with the rhythmic melody of music which emerges through the metre of the stanzas and couplets . . . the imagery has to come through sharp and clear.

Sometimes I found myself comparing my situation with the one that I was in when I was twenty-seven years old, when I served two years in prison.* I wasn't in prison for offences against the person, but against property. I'd been living rough in those days, and took to breaking into factory canteens and the like to get food. It never occurred to me then that I needn't have stolen – I could have done what I was doing now, living off Nature. But hindsight only comes when you look back over your shoulder. The tent that I was now living in was much more cramped than the narrow cell I had to occupy, the food supply less certain and regular,

* Described in *A Cage of Shadows*, Hutchinson, 1973.

71

laundry more haphazard. But there were no custodians to order me about, no insistent company trying to claim my ears and attention when I didn't want to be bothered, no regimented marching to and from the mail-bag shops. Here in the woods I was as free as man could ever be. The keep-in walls were as far away as I wanted them to be, the rattle of keys and locks didn't exist . . . 'free' society and the society of prison seemed centuries away in the past, as if they had never been part of me. I say 'part of me' because I'd never really felt myself part of them. I was always an onlooker, never really a participant. I went through the motions which were expected of me.

I used to write 'poetry' in prison. Anguished yelpings in rhyme. Fists of words knocking on an iron-studded door, asking to be let out. Notebooks and pencils were rationed, and my output of scribblings had a bigger appetite than the ration. So I had to cramp the writing into small, minute words, making a single notebook serve the purpose of half a dozen. When filled, the books were handed in to the prison censor who would decide whether or not you could take them away with you at discharge. There was a printed warning in the front cover of each notebook forbidding you to write anything derogatory about the prison, its officers and staff and what have you. Neither could you write anything about the offences which had brought you to the dark gloomy prison, or about any other prisoners, the food, the smells, or again what have you. I used to think, even then, that the Home Office as usual was still riding in the convict ships of old, galloping to nowhere with the Bow Street Runners. By allowing men to write their true thoughts into their notebooks and then analysing the contents, they'd probably have learned more about crime and its causes than the entire payroll of aftercare and social workers, and probation officers.

But at least prison had taught me how to make and use tinder and steel, which we used 'inside' to light our slim hand-rolled cigarettes, and how to dry leaves to serve as tobacco. In the prison exercise yards were the odd shrubs or sad-looking trees doing life imprisonment, and it was a simple enough matter to snatch a few leaves as I walked the circle. Necessity is usually the spur to innovation, discovery and invention. When I wrote on my birch-bark patches, handwriting once again cramped and small formed, I could see myself back in the cell doing the same thing. But there I tried to write in an atmosphere of stone-chilled frowns, smells of carbolic soap, odours of bad drains and sewer boshes, sweat of men, clash of boots on iron causeways and catwalks. Here I could write in peace, especially at nighttime with the fire blazing and the stars winking encouragement and approval. No longer a case of 'sleep faster, we need the pillows'. Everything now seemed slow paced, unurgent, untrembling.

From the tree line of the woods where my tent was pitched I could see out over three meadows, each separated from the other by flanks of hedges but with a gateway leading from one to the other. As the weeks passed and the weather permitted, I'd sit at the edge of the wood and gaze out across the meadows. Sometimes they were sharp but mellow in autumn sunlight, other times they were vague and mysterious with restless mist drifting across them. The Romans had come this way almost two thousand years ago but could not penetrate the great forest tracts of land which covered the area now called the Black Country, whose forests have long been cut down to feed the iron-smelters'· furnaces. My mind's eye painted the legions coming through the mist, over the meadows, could hear the chariots of the officers, the marching tread of the foot soldiers as they veered near and then away towards Lichfield.

The first meadow, the one nearest to me, always seemed to be the most nature busy. Rabbits foraged there, and the birds seemed to favour it. Several times I saw a fox crossing its acres, slink-hugging the ground. Crows, noisy black bullies, dominated like hoarse broken exhaust pipes on mopeds. The second meadow seemed only populated by birds; so was the third. And gradually I came to realize that the first meadow was the safest for the four-legged wild life, and only the more adventurous would go to the second. Very, very rarely did I see a four-legged creature in the third meadow, where the pickings must have been richer.

It was a sparrow hawk that gave me the clue. He'd glide in from a good height, stand wing-still on the air twenty feet or so above the ground, then drop at menacing speed. He'd swoop, pounce, then lift into the sky again with some small creature gripped between his talons. The moment he swooped, his shadow larger than life against the sunlit earth, the rabbits would bolt for cover, their cottonwool tails bobbing in panic, their hind legs drumming a tattoo of warning to others of their kind. As they bobtailed it for the safety of the woods they set up a chain reaction of alarm, causing birds to scatter skywards, and fieldmice to plunge and plough earthwards. General panic in the first meadow; but the woods offered safety, and that's why they didn't range into the second or third – the run from danger would be too far.

'In all animals, me lover,' Konk told me, 'habit bist the crust round self-survival. Man's an animal, only he don't like admitting it – he likes to call *his* habits by flattering names like, er, calling 'em "personality mannerisms" or "applied intelligence" or someat . . . honestly I'm telling thee, I don't know who dreams the names up . . .'

I got to thinking that people, myself included, are like that – that most of us are First Meadow people, scared to range too far because of the unknown. We stay with the safety of the tree line, the safety of the woods. The safety of convention – the mass of us are First Meadow dwellers; only a few range into the Second Meadow, and fewer still into the Third . . . the meadows of mental and spiritual experience. The mass of us wants the safety of the woods to run to, the safe familiar things. We deny that labels apply to us, we're apt to pretend that we're 'individuals', unique. But the sad truth is that we're mostly duplicates of one another, milling around for our lifespans inside the First Meadow. Sometimes we catch a glimpse of the Second Meadow and hesitate whether or not we should pass through the gate; and whilst we hesitate we are swept past it by the milling throng and are left with some vague discontent . . . some yearning because we have lost an opportunity to gain a new experience of unutterable value. Do we see vague shapes in that Second Meadow as we swirl past, and echo the words of James Elroy Flecker. . . ?

Since I can never see your face,
And never shake you by the hand,
I send my soul through time and space
To greet you. You will understand.

Does the still deepness of each of us sob with yearning because we know the gate is there but we have no way of opening it?

Perhaps a few people do ignore the pressing throng, struggle against the mass with instinctive and increasing determination, and do pass through the gate. And maybe, eventually, a few of those few see the gate which leads into the Third Meadow and pass through that. I wonder, is there yet another meadow, and another . . . and are the people dwelling there lonely because they are so thinly populated, or happy because only the true seeds of creative goodness have entered . . . or are they locked away in First Meadow lunatic asylums because they are considered 'strange' . . . irresponsible, mad, unbalanced?

I often asked myself who had passed through the gate leading into the Second Meadow – the great thinkers and poets, painters and music-makers? Yes, these *must* have passed through. Who then had passed into the Third if it be there – and *surely* it must be there? Christ, Plato, Beethoven? The few precious people who had stood upon great mountain peaks above all others, those rare geniuses who were linked together but separated by the distance of centuries?

Yes, I thought, these above all had at least passed into the Second Meadow, and perhaps into the Third. New uncluttered mental and spiritual pastures . . . voyagers of the universe within . . .

As a child I remember looking at a powdered-milk packet. Printed on the box was the picture of a woman holding a baby and on the table by which she sat there was a powdered-milk packet with the picture of a woman holding a baby and on the table was a powdered-milk packet . . . and the picture went on and on, like a hall of mirrors, into impossibility. Or so it seemed to me.

Sitting at the edge of the wood I thought of the milk-packet pictures and wondered if *that* were a symbol and glimpse of the Second Meadow, and, once inside, other meadows of the mind and senses opened up in the same way. But no, it couldn't be. The milk-packet pictures were only duplicates of one another, so my childhood impression of exciting mystery was a First Meadow one after all. The repeated, diminishing pictures told nothing new; gave no extra dimension to the senses, only repeated themselves. They provided an illusion, a delusion, and not a truth. They were not an insight but a death; because the novelty and cleverness of the duplicated pictures caused confusion and killed insight. Yet again, Old Konk cross-faded into my mind.

'It's life, me lover. The mouse poisons the pantry, the cat kills the mouse, the dog kills the cat – it goes on like that for ever . . .'

So even the innocence of childhood is rooted in the First Meadow . . . the key to the gate of the Second Meadow must therefore lie in wisdom and not in innocence . . . and there's the shame, I think, for what is purer than child innocence?

Living alone as I was doing amongst the woods and meadows I gradually became aware that personal inconsistencies loomed so large that I could hardly see them for size. It was mid October when I met Penny. Penny was a wood pigeon – I gave her the name – and I found her in the first meadow near to my woods, flapping around and crying with a damaged wing. I picked her up and saw that the damage wasn't too bad, but enough to prevent her from getting airborne for a while. A single shotgun ball was lodged in the leading edge of one of her wings. I held the pigeon in my hands, wondering whether to finish her off and plonk her in the pot, then decided there wasn't a lot of meat to her. But I think this was a Second Meadow thought and impulse, the decision that I didn't want to destroy her. My aloneness was bordering upon loneliness. So I took Penny back to camp and carefully removed the pellet, then bathed the injury in warm water and put a smear of grease on it to keep the dirt out. Then I shut her inside the tent whilst I collected twigs and briars to make a crude but comfortable cage, lining the floor with bracken to keep her warm of nights.

She became my close companion for over a week, and it did cross my mind that I could use her to good purpose and advantage. If I were to trim her flight feathers and peg her out on a tether stick she'd act as a living decoy to bring the plump cock birds down to rifle shot. I toyed seriously with the idea, then admitted to myself that she'd become my friend and I didn't want to make her betray her own kind. But equally, her own kind kept her alive. As I shot pigeons for the pot I opened their craws and removed the undigested food which I fed to Penny. It was all a bit daft and hypocritical, really. Every time I ate pigeon I shut Penny's cage inside the tent so that she couldn't see me eating her relatives and kin. I felt like a half-converted cannibal still having a crafty gnaw at a human limb when the missionaries weren't looking.

When her wing was strong again I took her from her cage and let her go. She tested herself against the wind, then soared away.

'Go find another meadow, Penny,' I called after her. 'I'll not recognize you among the other birds, and like as not you'll fall to my gun.'

She flew away, and the pup-tent seemed empty without her.

'A bird in the hand's worth two in the sky,' Konk's voice

scolded at me. 'Now like as not she'll go and tell t'others to keep out'n your road. Pigeons bisn't stupid, me lover.'

Animals and birds are peculiar creatures, I got to thinking. If they remain anonymous you shoot and eat them without a second thought. Once you've made pets of them, you'll do almost anything to save them from pain and danger. If I kept sheep and a stranger's dog worried them, I'd shoot it; if my own dog worried them I'd scold it, punish it, but doubt I could kill it. Living alone and remote from human companionship you find memories coming to the surface of your mind where you can read them like a picture book. Sitting near the fire with the blanket of night shrouding in, eating flame-roasted pheasant and rabbit, ripples of amusement came back to me.

I'd once done a radio chat show about poaching and as a result was invited back onto the air to argue the merits of poaching with a titled landowner who, amongst other things, bred pheasants for American syndicates to come over and shoot at around £200 per gun per day. I remember that the argument raged hotly, the landowner complaining bitterly that it cost him thousands of pounds to stock his land with game whilst men of my ilk came onto his land and stole the game. I argued back that he'd got no damned right to the land anyway, unless it were under the plough for general food production, and furthermore his ancestors had stolen the common land from mine. He reflected regretfully that it was a pity I hadn't been around just over a hundred years ago, when men like me would have been transported to the Australian prison colonies for at least seven years for stealing game. Probably executed if found with a gun. The way he said it, I think he wished they'd bring the transportation laws back. The interviewer summed up at the end of the chat show.

'Now, Archie, you've heard Lord Blank say how much it cost him to stock his land – aren't you ashamed of the poaching you've done, and the poaching that still goes on?'

'I am ashamed,' I answered. 'I'm bloody well ashamed that

there aren't more poachers to take from him what his sires took from us.'

The interview–chat ended friendlily enough, with the land-owner throwing down a challenge for me to go to his land and try to get past his keepers. I accepted the challenge readily, then made careful preparations for my mission. He'd be expecting me, that was for certain, and poaching calls for cunning as well as for skill. I regarded the challenge itself as the main clause and the methods of taking his birds as secondary. In other words, the results were to count, and not the means.

I borrowed some equipment from a radio-broadcasting friend; a portable Uher tape recorder and a 'loofah' micro-phone – this was about four feet long and twelve inches in diameter, the outer skin of the casing having the feel and texture of a bathroom loofah. I removed the innards from the microphone, leaving the inside free enough to place my .410 single-barrelled shotgun inside. This was a real poacher's piece which split into two halves, so that the barrel could be suspended under one arm and the butt under the other. A loose-fitting jacket would amply conceal the gun if necessary. I also borrowed from my friend a tape of bird-songs. I added a pair of fieldglasses to my kit and set off for 'gentry land'. I booked in at a small village inn for a few days, a mile or so from the place where I intended to lift the pheasants. The first two mornings and evenings I drove to the top of the hill which overlooked the land, and through my fieldglasses could mark the spots where the pheasants had their feeding grounds, the places where the keepers put food out. Satisfied, I then discreetly sought out the pub where the keepers were wont to pop in for the odd pint or two. I draped a camera round my neck to make out that I was a tourist passing through. When I saw two of the keepers come into the taproom together, youngish men, I immediately marked them as 'range-rover cowboys'. There was very little dust on their boots, or even caked mud, to start with. Not like the old-time keepers, I thought. These just ride round the estate on four wheels, like a police panda-car crew ... and in no way can you better the 'man on the beat', covering his bailiwick on the two pistons known as legs which Mother Nature provided him with.

'College education knocks all the bloody common sense out'n 'em,' Old Konk muttered to me. 'They'm so busy these days getting hold of bits of paper called "Degrees" that most of 'em can hardly tell a pheasant from a kestrel, ah've bin thinking. And they gets paid for not knowing, as well.'

I took my birds early next morning, just before the first streaks of dawn were unzipping the sky's sleeping bag.

I parked my car on a grass verge with a note under the wiperblade saying that it had broken down and the owner was seeking out a garage, and walked to the pheasant woods with tape recorder strapped over one shoulder and the shotgun concealed inside the loofah. If I *were* surprised by the keepers I intended to bluff it out by saying that I was recording birdsongs for a broadcast. The songs already on the tape would lend authentic support to my claim ... but nobody interrupted me, I wasn't sprung. I dropped three brace of perching pheasants in less than twenty minutes, the slight snorting cough of the .410 being swallowed up by the thickets and trees. I retraced my footsteps to the car, took the birds back to the inn with me – myself smugly satisfied – and had breakfast. At the more respectable hour of 10.30 I drove up to Lord Blank's house and rang the front door bell. A servant opened up to me, looking with surprise at the brace of birds I held. Lord Blank was equally surprised as I made him a present of his own birds, but he was amused too. We sat and yarned a bit, him over a very early morning sherry and me over coffee. We parted the best of friends, and remain so. Two of the pheasants I gave to my broadcaster friend, the other two I kept for myself.

It's only when I returned the equipment to my friend that we suddenly realized that the recorded birdsongs were of South American birds which never visited this country ... I wonder if the gamekeepers would have known that, had they sprung me. If they had, I think I would have bluffed it out by swearing blind that they were the songs of specially bred Black Country pit canaries.

News of the pheasant venture got around. A television producer phoned me up.

'We want to do a piece on rabbit poaching,' he said. 'Can you fix it up? I want to bring a camera crew out to you.'

I said, yes, I could fix it up, but it wouldn't be poaching in the strict sense, not with a camera crew herding all over the place. He'd have to get permission from a farmer whose name I gave to him. He got the permission, and I paddocked in an old poacher friend of mine who'd got some good polecat ferrets and a good lurcher dog. Plus purse nets. When the camera crew arrived on the scene, I was amazed. Three carloads of people – sixteen in all – and a huge van full of equipment. Director, producer, first and second cameramen, recordists, continuity staff, clapperboard boy, this, that and the other.

'We're going to catch a couple of rabbits,' I observed in a yelp. 'Not make a bloody epic film about Cleopatra.'

Two hours went by, and we hadn't sighted a single rabbit.

'Not doing very well, are we?' the producer asked.

'No wonder at it, with you lot wallowing about like elephants in heat. You're keeping the rabbits pinned down in their buries – and one of our ferrets as well. They won't come out because they think there's a thunderstorm overhead. Quietness is the essence of this job.'

He shrugged, glanced at his watch.

'We'll nip off and find a place to get a lunch snack,' he said. 'Let things quieten down a bit, and you can encourage some of the rabbits to come out.'

I watched them straggle away towards their cars. Imagine being on a tiger hunt with that lot, I thought; 'We'll just sit on the grass and have a quiet smoke, my good man, while you nip off and catch a tiger.'

'What'll we do?' my poacher friend asked. 'We'll get nothing this way.'

'Sit on the grass and have a smoke,' I answered. 'I'll be back in a jiffy.' I drove swiftly to a butcher's shop in a nearby hamlet, bought two unskinned and ungutted rabbits off him, and raced back to the location. My friend had retrieved the missing ferret. I handed him the two dead rabbits.

'Stick 'em behind a couple of the purse nets,' I told him. 'Just leave 'em inside the bury holes where they can't be seen. Then put a ferret down and "find" the rabbits when the cameras are rolling.'

So that's what we did. When the crew returned and took another hour or so to set up their equipment and get the lighting right, we 'caught' a couple of rabbits for them. My poacher friend pretended to snap their necks as he hauled them out – the way he did it, making the dead animals jerk in his hands as if they were alive, made him a good candidate for an acting role in 'Emmerdale Farm'. The television people were jubilant. They'd seen and filmed Nature in the raw; they'd lived recklessly and dangerously, and the rabbits hadn't fought back.

'Three hundred pounds okay for you?' the producer asked me. 'And say fifty for your friend?'

'It'll do,' I answered nonchalantly. 'Send his cheque direct to him, send mine via my agent. D'you want one of the rabbits?'

He shuddered. 'No thanks. Can't stand the things.'

I gave one to my friend and kept the other. That night I made a rabbit stew and, as my wife and son and I ate it I did a quick mental calculation. A full day spent with a filming crew of sixteen; wages, travelling expenses, cost of film, developing, printing, editing, the use of equipment . . .

'Scoff it down and enjoy it,' I told my family. 'You'll never have another like it. It's cost about two thousand pounds, this meal has.'

Six

Checking my traps for snared rabbits or going after them with my rifle, I often wished I'd got a good dog with me. Not only for the companionship of it, but for its usefulness. Some people prefer lurchers or labradors, particularly retrievers, when out in the field. I prefer a good blooded Staffordshire bull terrier. Most huntsmen would laugh at the idea of taking such a dog along for gun use, but I reckon that one man's dog is another man's laugh. Train what you prefer, and if you start early enough, from puppyhood, you can train almost any dog to the field. Train them to be alert, quiet, to nose-point the direction the game lies in, and to fetch with a gentle-enough mouth. What more could you ask for? I prefer a Stafford bull terrier because of its looks, the affection it returns, its spirit and guts, and its loyal intelligence. My native Black Country favours the Stafford bull terrier, above all men of my generation do. Perhaps the younger men would prefer to keep a poodle for the wife, or a Jack Russell, that sort of thing. OK as pets, maybe. Nothing much else to them. I suppose high-rise flats and official regulations governing the keeping of dogs on post-war council estates has a lot to do with it.

Way back in the shanty-town days of the Industrial Revolution, with cholera ever a-visiting and the life span of the average man around twenty-four years, bull-baiting was a festive occasion attended by gentry and common man alike – and it was the Stafford bull terrier which was invariably put in to pin the bulls. The 'game' was officially outlawed in 1826, but it covertly lingered on for many a long year afterwards. Life was bitter and hard in the region of my ancestors, so no wonder its men played hard and bitter too. Yet – much as the outsider might frown on and condemn this brutal 'sport' – it's worth keeping in mind that before bull-baiting became an actual sport it had been illegal to butcher a bull and offer its meat up for sale if it *hadn't* been baited by dogs. Only baited meat could be sold, so no wonder crowds collected to watch the baiting and to place bets on the side, betting one dog against another. This way they could actually see the condition of the beef they would be paying for and eating, and the butcher couldn't palm them off with old stringy beef which had died of old age or disease. It was generally believed that when an animal died following great physical exertion the meat was more tender – and many people still maintain today that coursed hares are more tender than any other. Although in the very early days it was the butcher who arranged the actual baiting of his bull, it wasn't long before the populace started to do it on their own. The Black Country is full of placenames bearing evidence of the sport; the Bull Ring in Birmingham, the Bull Stakes at Sedgley and Darlaston are but three. The bull was usually tethered to a twenty-foot rope, and the dogs put to him, mostly one or two at a time. The dog was trained to go for the nose or jowls, or the underlip – and hang on. The idea was for the winning dog to hang onto the bull until the beast tired and fell to its knees. The bull was then classed as 'pinned' and the dog which pinned him won stake monies for its owner. We might as well say 'steak monies' and expose the pun. Quite often, the bull terriers had literally to be cut away from the bull. I suppose the baiting of the bulls was legally stopped when the men took to baiting any farmer's bull they saw in a field, taking away the operation from the jurisdiction of the appointed butcher.

It was only in the latter part of the thirties that the Stafford bull terrier was given official status as a dog (as if it mattered) by Crufts. Specimens of the breed were put up year after year, but were rejected by the eyes of official recognition. Perhaps they thought that a dog highly esteemed by the common man wasn't worth considering by the privileged elite. The story goes – and I for one won't gainsay it – that one man who tried to get official recognition for the breed was curtly ordered to go away.

'Take that cur out of here – go on, get it out.'

'Why? Whass-a matter with it?'

'Its legs are too short, for one thing.'

'Whass-a matter wi' his bloody legs? They reachen the bloody floor, don' they?'

A good Stafford stands eighteen inches to the shoulders, weighs forty pounds in fighting trim, and keeps his ears at prick when being shown. But he's got the sense to lay them back from prick when he's not being shown, in case another dog has a go at him and uses his ears to get his teeth into. Another quality about the Stafford which endears him to me is that no matter how much he loves his master, if his master lays hands on his children or wife, it's to their defence the dog will go. As if he senses that they are weaker and need his protection, no matter the divided loyalty he obviously feels. A good dog to have, is a Stafford bull. Not the prettiest, but the most loyal and tough, bar none. They're popular with American huntsmen, too, although the Americans like to breed them with long legs, so that they stand almost high as a Great Dane.

My father told me that when I was a baby he had a Stafford bull terrier that kept him, my Mam and the police at bay for two hours. They'd gone shopping and left me outside a shop, telling the dog to 'guard' me. The dog sat down near the pram and wouldn't let anyone near me, not even Mom and Dad. The police eventually put a net over the dog whilst Mom wheeled my pram away, leaving Dad to re-gentle it. Was Dad's fault, really. He'd given the order 'On guard, boy' when the pram was outside the shop, but hadn't cancelled the order when he came out. He'd just tried to wheel the pram away, expecting the dog to follow at his heels. If he'd have said 'Good boy, all right now. Heel,' the dog would have understood what was expected of him. It's very seldom a good dog is confused on its own; it's people who confuse him.

Yes, it would have been nice to have had a dog with me there in the woods. There was more than enough meat for the two of us. I checked my rabbit snares – 'hingles' we really called them – every evening and early morning, getting to whatever I'd caught before the stoats or weasels did. One day while going out to inspect the traps I actually caught a hare by hand. No trap, no gun, just my hands. It was squatting on a mound of earth, part covered by a clump of grass, the resting hare's favourite position so that he can see all points of the compass. I walked past him at about ten yards distance, pretending I hadn't seen him. This made the hare feel secure; he stayed where he was, firm and still, so as not to attract my attention. Or so he thought. I walked on towards a line of hedges in front of him, taking my anorak off as I went. I casually hung the anorak from a thorn peg and passed through the hedges, then quietly looped round in a half circle until I was at the rear of the hare again. He still sat there, staring at my coat hanging from the hedge. I walked up to the hare, still pretending that I didn't know he was there, and whilst he was puzzling it out I bent down swiftly as I passed him and caught him by the ears. One swift blow and he was ready for the pot.

Old Konk loved to eat hare. He'd got his own grandparents' hand-me-down recipes for jugging them, roasting them, stewing them, and he'd never let on what the ingredients were. He chose his herbs with care too, taken from the fields and hedgerows, as the hares were. He could make a meal fit for a king. Give Konk the choice of a single hare or six brace of pheasants on a poaching trip, and ten to one he'd settle for the hare. He and a particular farmer were always having running battles with each other, because the farmer was fond of jugged hare, too, and felt that his land didn't stock enough for him and Konk both. Whenever Konk was abroad with his dog, the farmer slipped his own bitches free, let them run loose so's to draw Konk's dog away. Dog nature is pretty much like human nature where sex is concerned. You can't expect a healthy mature dog to concentrate on hare-hunting when bitches in heat are throwing invitations across the winds. The farmer knocked nails into the underside of his gates and fences where hares passed through, to damage Konk's nets when he placed them. Or he'd plait thorn briars in position to serve the same purpose. When Konk came upon the sabotaged spots, he'd mark them with a couple of pigeon feathers and then avoid them. The two men were as bitter as chewed conkers towards each other. Daft, really, because there was enough feathered fruit around for both of them, had they reached an amicable agreement. But, as Konk often said, the farmer was so mean and miserable that even his cows came under his influence and only gave sour milk.

The farmer liked his drink on a Saturday night, though, and always took a skinful of wallop. He'd put on his best suit and bowler hat, harness the pony to the trap, and spank off to the pub a mile and a half away. At the end of the evening's session, the publican would support him, blind drunk and ready for bed, back into the trap and point the pony homewards. The pony knew the way blindfold – it was Saturday night out for him as well as for the farmer. Off he'd go at a gentle soothing walk, the farmer snoring in a huddled-up lump on the driving seat, and once the trap clattered into the cobbled yard of the farm, wife and eldest son would come out and lift drunken father into the house. The drill had been the same for years.

Konk and Dad interrupted it. Made it break step, as it were. They waited in the lane between farm and pub until they saw the trap coming homewards. They quietly stopped the pony by a five-barred gate and uncoupled it. They took the pony into the field and shut the gate on it. Then, without waking the farmer, they eased the shafts of the trap through the gate bars and then rehitched the pony to it. And that's how they left it. God knows what the farmer thought when he woke up and saw a five-barred gate between him and his pony and half of his trap. Perhaps it cured him of heavy weekend drinking, because it must have been one hell of a shock to his alcohol-battered system.

Since the myxomatosis epidemic was introduced from the Continent into this country in 1953 the deep warren burrows which were common in English countryside have almost disappeared. Rabbits now tend to burrow and nest shallowly. They seem to be smaller, too, as if returning genetically to their ancestors, the coneys brought here by the Normans. Myxi caused a slow, awful death to the creatures, like a sort of gangrene eating them away and causing their eyes to swell into blindness. But now they seem to have found immunity from the plague and have multiplied again. Yet, because of their shallow 'stops' which they live and breed in, they fall more readily as prey to foxes and stoats, and as a result of man's interference in the pattern of Nature these predators flourish the more. I wonder why man keeps fiddling around with Nature's fuse box when he knows so little about her energy fields.

From gun to traps, from fungi to food plants, I ate well and hearty. But fishing eluded me – I only caught three fish in all. Fair-sized ones and enjoyable to eat, but I just couldn't get the hang of fishing no matter how much I tried. I've heard of poachers catching trout by hand, by tickling them, but I think it's an old wives' tale. I've met many a one who claims to have met somebody who's done it, but never a body who has *personally* done it. As for spearing fish by torchlight – 'burning the water' – I suppose it could be done if the eye were keen enough to allow for the light refraction, or if the spearer were wearing polarized glasses. Better to find a well-stocked lake and take a small boy with a toy boat to it, and dangle baited hooks from the keel as Konk and Dad did with me. I *have* seen fish caught by using a sledgehammer: the man stood upon a rock in the middle of a stream and scattered bait seed round the base and which the fish came to eat he just slammed the hammer hard against the rock he was standing on, then netted the fish in. They were stunned by the shock waves. The man said he got the idea while serving in the Spanish Civil War of 1937, when the rations were slow in coming up. He and his mates used to toss hand grenades into the fish streams or lakes, then scoop in the dead and concussed fish.

Today, many modern fish 'poachers' use chemicals. A sackful of chlorate of lime poured into the water will kill all the fish in a hundred-yard stretch. Poaching as an art has almost completely waned. Today, a couple of trucks will drive down the motorways, turn off into the country somewhere, and the 'cowboys' will stop and drop the tailboards near a field and rustle half a dozen calves or bullocks, then high-tail it back to the concrete canyon cities and make a handsome profit. I heard tell of two men from a city who drove out into the country in a luxurious car, each equipped with shotguns – one actually a Purdy – and fired at game through the open windows of the car. The village bobby came along (there *are* still some about) on his bicycle and spotted them. They quickly dropped their guns into a ditch alongside where they were parked on the verge. They told the policeman they were having a rest and a smoke before driving on to London.

'You been shooting?' the policeman asked. 'I heard shooting.'

'No, not us. We're just having a rest.'

'Got any guns with you?'

'No. We haven't any guns. Search the car, if you like.'

'You sure you haven't any guns?'

'Quite sure, officer. We have no guns.'

The policeman climbed into the ditch, then out again, holding the two guns.

'I can see that you're gentlemen,' he said, 'and wouldn't lie to a police officer. It's a lucky coincidence that you parked where you did, otherwise I wouldn't have found these beauties. You must have frightened the poachers away, and they left their guns behind. Well, it's an ill wind that blows no good . . . these guns will be mine if nobody has claimed them by three months' time.'

So much for the 'cowboy' poachers riding about on four wheels. It's been recorded somewhere that a particular poacher turned up at a large estate one day when he knew that the owner was absent. He turned up early on a particular October the 1st, the day when the pheasant-shooting season officially opens. The landowner had postponed the opening up of his own and his friends' guns for a day, his business in London being so urgent. The poacher, a stranger to the area, had got wind of this on the grapevine. This was in the days when horse and trap were more common than motorcars. He turned up at the keeper's lodge carrying a brace of twelve-bores, cased, and dressed for the occasion in hired shooting togs. The keeper was surprised to see him, but the cheeky poacher-cum-con man won him over.

'Morning, my man. Your master's expecting me. Sorry I'm a bit late, but my horse cast a shoe near the village and I've left my own man to take it to the blacksmith. Will you take me to the others, and I'll get started.'

'The master's not here, sir. He's put the shoot off till to-morrow.'

'What's that you say? Put the shoot *off*? Master not here? But he told me to come this morning, and a dickens of a way I've come.'

'I'm sorry, sir . . . but that's the way on it. He was called away sudden, like.'

'M'mm, no wonder he couldn't let me know, then. Anyway, I'm here now. You might as well beat for me and I'll let a few barrels off so's I needn't call it a wasted day. You can tell your master I've been and that I can't get back for the shoot tomorrow. I'll leave you my card to give him.'

'Very good, sir. I'll get my boy to give a hand, and one of my junior keepers. One of 'em can reload for you, if that's all right, sir.'

'That's all right with me, my man. There's a sovereign each for them if we get a good bag. How many guns coming tomorrow?'

'About thirty, sir.'

'Oh well. We'll leave plenty for them to nibble at, eh?'

By all accounts, the poacher–con man didn't leave such a large nibble at that. By the time he'd decided to put his guns up and rest his aching shoulder he'd got a mountain of pheasants, all collected in by the keeper and his assistant and their dogs. He'd got a fair-sized mountain of feathered fruit.

'We'll collect them up if you'll fetch some handcarts,' he told the two men and the lad. 'Go up to the house first and tell the cellar man to give you some beer. You've earned it. Send a message to her ladyship I'll be along in a while.'

The moment he was alone, the cheeky sod whistled up the two cronies he'd got waiting with horses and traps along the lane, and soon they were away at a spanking pace despite being laden down with pheasants.

It's strange to ponder upon the fact that our modern police force owes much to the old-time gamekeeper and poacher. They formed the ranks of the Bow Street Runners who gradually merged into Robert Peel's 'Bobbies'; poachers and gamekeepers were men skilled in the arts of tracking, observation, the interpretation of human nature as well as that of animals and creatures. They had the inbuilt ability to use the mind's eyes of instinct.

Thoughts, memories, hunting, writing with birch bark and fungi ink, all filled so much of my time that the hours from sun-up to sun-down seemed all too short. The autumn had now well and truly set in, but so gradually that I hardly noticed it. I had warm clothing, waterproofs, and no chink had appeared in the canvas of my tent. Some mornings I woke up to early frost, crystal sharp and crackling under foot, and sometimes to mists which draped tendrils round the trees and patchworked the fields in strange grey-whiteness. Even in the bitterest frosts food presented no problem. Nature provided an all-the-year-round larder of shepherd's purse ('pick-pocket' we called it in my childhood) and I used the chopped leaves as cabbage. I'd got chickweed either to boil as a vegetable or to eat raw as a salad. There was cleavers – 'hug-me-close', 'goosegrass' – which plant stood me in good stead when the frosts were really heavy and little else could be distinguished above ground. I boiled this up as a spinach. Dock leaves cooked well with meat, and were also good to wrap round uncooked meat to keep it fresh and insect-free. To make a change from acorn and dandelion-leaf coffee I used crushed wintergreen leaves to make tea. The wintergreen leaves also provided vegetable salad food. Tansy, a fern-leafed tallish herb, gave me a good lemon-scented flavouring, as did the marjoram – some of the leaves I dried in with the wintergreen to make the tea more 'solid'. For the picking and using of much of the wild plant life I had to rely upon memory and common sense, since I'm not a particularly clued-up naturalist. But, as my Dad used to say, you can't go wrong unless you do . . .

Hazelnuts were well ripened by the end of September and into November, but they needed keen eyes and patience to seek them out against the leaf hues of autumn. I merely let the squirrels lead me to them. I knew that weight for weight hazelnuts housed 50 per cent more protein and seven times more fat and carbohydrate than hens' eggs, so no wonder the squirrels I shot around this time were plump and fat. Then I'd got sweet chestnuts, a real private harvest of them, which I could eat raw, roasted, or chopped up and boiled into a purée to pour over my meat. It was good to sit and roast them by the fire on a frosty night. I'd slit the skins and put them into the glowing fire, except for one which I didn't slit. When this popped and exploded, I knew that the others were ready for eating. They gave off a rich welcoming smell, a smell the colour of contentment.

Smell . . . perhaps the most sensitive of our five senses, conjuring in an instant the fulsomeness of things which happened long ago. The smell of roasting chestnuts from my campfire brought back the smell of baked bread   baked bread and a cold frosty night . . . it was the early years of the 1930s and I hadn't as yet started school. There was myself, an elder sister, and two young brothers. At this time we lived in a small cottage-type house at a place called Kinver, almost within shouting distance of my campsite where I was now roasting chestnuts. Kinver was a paradise of a place for a child to grow up in. The sloping hills, the valleys, the pine trees. In the near distance the profiles of Shropshire spreading sweetly to the eyes on the one horizon, and on the other the brooding scowls of the industrial Black Country, chafing away towards Birmingham. But I can still smell the memories of Kinver's valleys. The smells of the four seasons, each with their different scents. The newness of each spring and the ripeness of the advancing summers; the almost sad mellowness of autumns and the brisk airs and frosts and snows of winter. Winters I particularly remember because the wind seemed to wind itself down the chimney and cry for warmth. The wind seemed so lonely; it seemed to me as a child that it was looking for company and for comfort. I felt sorry for the wind because I had no way of talking back to it. So it had to talk and moan to itself inside the dark chimney.

My father was unemployed, as were so many in those prewar depression days, and there were no blankets of social security to cover the wound. Men used to squat in puddles on street corners, wondering what to do. Puzzling at the factors of politics, I think. So, to eke out the dole-money pittances my father used to go out of nights with Old Konk to poach small game for the table. Often they'd take me with them into the spinneys to set up the nets or to act as lookout. Sometimes they'd take a pair of polecat ferrets with them, a hob and a jill. The hob's the male, the jill's the female. Invariably they'd put the hob down the rabbit buries, knowing that he'd be anxious to get his work over and done with, and return to his mate topside. The smell of fur and feather always tugs at my senses, at my memories. The smell of damp woods and newly turned earth, or dry bracken strikes lovely

93

chords inside my mind. It's strange how memories cling to us, linger inside some compartment of the mind, forgotten on the surface until some small rippling echo brings them awake. Like a string plucked upon a harp which strikes a note, and from the note comes a melody, and the melody remains for ever in the memory.

For me, a particular memory is that of newly baked bread. It takes me back to over fifty years ago. There were only three rooms in our cottage, one down and two up. They were very small rooms, the downstairs one being the larger. This held a table, a few chairs, an old horsehair sofa and very little else except the cooking range. The floor of the kitchen-cum-living room was red quarried, thick heavy slabs of tile, with one or two home-made rugs scattered about. The cooking range was made of cast iron, with a central solid-fuel fireplace. An oven either side, and trivets which could be swung out over the open fire to hold the kettle or the cooking pots. Fuel for the fire was collected in from the nearby woodlands, sometimes supplemented by a bit of coal my father would steal from the canal wharf. He stole not because he was a thief in the true sense of the meaning but because of necessity; the driving force of a man providing for his family when times were often more impossible than merely hard. When 'hard times' meant survival at any price, at any cost. From time to time my Dad would disappear from home for a few weeks, and I'd wonder about this. In time I learned that he was doing short terms of imprisonment for poaching, or coal stealing, or taking potatoes from farmers' fields. Yet, whilst he was away, we seemed to manage – very frugally, I must admit, but there was always the kind poacher who'd leave a rabbit on the back step or a few fish taken from a private stream.

The hardness of a hard life didn't really hit us until one winter. It was cold, bitter cold, with long lonely winds moaning through the trees and wailing through the valleys. In the mornings, blue with cold, I'd go out to the tap in the yard with a spill of lighted paper to thaw the frozen waterpipe.

Jack-frost patterns in ice on the house windows, as thick as the glass itself. Wood fire crackling in the grate but seeming to throw out no heat. All of us huddling around in coats, blankets, anything to give warmth. And Dad was away from home. Whether he was in prison again or he'd gone on the tramp looking for work, I don't remember; I only know that he was away from home. It was so bitterly cold the other men couldn't get out to poach. I think even the rabbits would have frozen to death had they ventured out of their buries. Soon, with Dad absent, the little food we had in the house gave out. Creases of increasing worry frowned my mother's face. We cried out for more food, not understanding why she wouldn't give us any. Not wouldn't – couldn't. There was none to give.

Two days went by and we hadn't tasted a morsel of food, we cried with hunger pains, hunger that I still so vividly remember. On the third day my mother sat by the wood fire with her apron over her head, weeping. Then she stopped, stood up, put on her old but one-and-only coat and left the house. We sat there, waiting in misery until she came back. When she came, she carried three loaves of bread and a jar of beef dripping. Where she got them from, I never did find out. Perhaps she begged them from the baker's shop in the village, or maybe from a neighbour. I never did find out how she pulled off such a wonderful miracle. Everybody was on the scrounge in those days, so the generosity of shopkeepers had to be curtailed so that they themselves could survive. What I do remember is that the loaves were hard as iron – had there been enough of them, a house could have been built from them. Hard as bricks, they were. Gathered around her we all watched as she stood at the sink and soaked the loaves in water. Then she squeezed them pulp-dry and put them into the baking oven. Slowly the smell of baking bread filled the room, making our mouths water and our eyes grow big as our stomachs. When they were rebaked she took them from the oven and cut large thick crusty wedges which she smeared with the beef dripping. We wolfed the meal down.

The yeasty smell of the bread, the rich tasting goodness of the crust, the warmth and belly-filling moisture of it – I don't think anyone sat down to a more splendid, satisfying meal.

And now, half a century later, I can't pass a baker's shop without pausing and inhaling the richness of newly baked bread and sending my mind back along the years. I won't buy ready-wrapped bread. It has to be fresh, newly baked, unsliced. Then I can slowly chew away at the moist centre part of the slice, leaving the crust edges until last because that's where the best taste and smell linger. As I eat it, I'm a little boy again waiting for my Dad to come home, with frost on the window panes and the howling winds of winter crying to the outside world; and mixed up in it all is the memory-fragrance of three loaves of sweet-smelling rich crusty bread . . .

If I left my campfire and went to the highest point of where I was pitched, and climbed the highest tree there, I would be able to see Kinver and, with fieldglasses, the cottage-house we'd lived in, if it were still standing. Fifty and more years separated the then from the now, fifty years of world-journeyings, years of personal flotsam and jetsam, fulfilled ambitions and broken ones. The sand ran so swiftly through the hourglass of time; soon I shall be old, I thought, and what will I have achieved except age?

The fire beamed smiles of light against the mist-darkness, the roasting chestnuts cracked and chuckled like fragments of warm conversations, the trees sighed like contented men after work was done and muscles and sinews could relax. Life was indeed a dome of many-coloured glass . . . each colour a prism blending other colours into a wonderful, wonderful richness.

Seven

My mind was happy in the woods, but I never completely escaped from the society I'd stepped aside from for a little while. Thoughts were ever busy, sipping like a bee from one pollen-giving patch to the next. Strangely, perhaps, most of my thoughts lay in the distant past, years and years away. Maybe this was because I was so near to my birthplace, to the boyhood region which had given me roots. The woods I lived in must have, at one time, been part of the great forest tract which encompassed Cannock Chase and spread its fleece through my Black Country and then yonder to Shropshire, taking time off to spread here into Worcestershire. My great-great-grandfather must have known this area of the West Midlands when it was all rich with fields' harvests, and his generation was the last to see it so, where no change had come about since the days of the Romans. He would have looked out at a pastoral landscape where men worked in the fields and husbanded the rich topsoil, never dreaming that industrial needs and greeds would come with strange machines and rip the valley asunder. In the space of fifty years, from 1750 to 1800, the standards of future 'progress' would be set. An industrial revolution would take place which some people, myself included, might call a mutation. The world itself would never recover from this mutation–revolution and the day would come when it reaped the harvest of shortages, pollutions, and loss of identity. True, my dead ancestor could have looked out and witnessed some

97

little degree of man's mechanized industry. A few nail shops littered around, a few opencast coal pits, a glassworks or two. But the general panorama would have shown a health of fields, slopes of woodlands, cattle grazing in large numbers, and the river Stour threading its way as clear and clean as a Highland beck. Fish in the Stour, then; not a yellowness of chemical wastes poisoning miles of its waters. The air over the valley would then be clear and clean, and nature-natural. Inside fifty years it would be smoke and poison-filled, and the great forests would be ripped away to show black scars of coal mines and tacky-banks. The newly opened canals would make water roads from one black iron works to the next. Great cancers of coal, limestone, clay, iron ores would be forced from the ground leaving worse cancers behind. The land would lose its peace, would wince under the shock of it all, and never really recover.

His son, my great-grandfather, would never really know what his father's eyes had seen. He, the son, would accept the increasing sprawl of industrialism as his lot, as his heritage. But perhaps here and there, in deep recesses of his mind, a countryman's protest growled and rumbled. But generally speaking, he fitted in with the 'brave new world'. Perhaps he was too busy fighting for survival to witness consciously the destruction of one of the loveliest areas in the English counties. Anyway, he became one of the first generation of Black Country men. His father had been a Green Country man. It's significant to me in some slight way that there is no true black in Nature; black's unnatural to her. Green's her favourite colour.

Probably the biggest social change my great-grandfather noticed at a personal level was that his father wore breeches to the knees, where they were fastened with laces or strings or buttons. But he, the son, would wear trousers to the ankles, wide and flapping, and unease at the new fashion would cause working men like himself to put little straps under their knees to pinch the trousers in. He would have stood on the top of the highest hill, my great-grandfather, and inside the perimeter of the now dark valley he would have seen the smoke and fire glow of around forty thousand nail shops. Later to be called 'cottage industries' by the pen men of the day to conjure up pleasant visions of happy well-fed men and women and children, and ivy clinging to olde-worlde crofts; buxom wenches with light baskets full of some product called iron nails . . . buxom wenches and healthy lads evidently picking nail fruits from orchard trees . . .

It wasn't like that. It was grim. A gruesome spectre to haunt the pages of history for ever. The green trees were felled in this region and the dark forests of back-to-back slums took their places, poking up from the ground like rotting teeth stumps in festering black gums. The houses were cages, bolt holes, dens and lairs in which to pen the work fodder, the slaves of industry. Negroes in slave plantations knew greater freedom than my kin ancestors. The old ways of life went away and the areas they'd dwelt in became covered in a dankness of factory stacks, furnaces and clanking machinery which stank and belched at the sun. Acres of dry brickyards, and the droop of men's spirits mixed in with the outpour of their sweat.

My great-great-grandfather would have awakened, as I did now, to the call of birds and the lowing of cattle, of sleepy winds soughing in the branches. He could have encompassed the area, my birthplace whose boundary I was camped on, in a day's ride on horseback. He could have mounted saddle in Stourbridge and moved at a slow trot to Wolverhampton, stopped there for a glass of ale in what was then no more than a small village. Then on to Willenhall. He might have dismounted there to relieve his bladder of the beer he'd drunk, then rode on to Walsall. Then the bridlepath to West Bromwich, and packhorse trail to Oldbury, which was less than a pinprick on the Ordnance maps of the day, if that. From here he would have posted saddle to Halesowen, perhaps turned to look back along the turnpike road which twisted up Mucklow's Hill and led to Birmingham. Then on to journey's end at Stourbridge again. On his ride he would have seen patches and thatches of villages, small homestead farms, and felt the quiet serenity as seen today in landscape paintings by Constable. If his ghost were still riding and he took it into his head to keep on going, he could be with me inside the hour to share my campfire and my supper. He, Konk and I would get along fine.

I feel, always, some chill of horror to think that the great open cleanliness of my great-great-grandfather's Green Country could have given way, in the space of a hundred years or so, to what my own eyes had seen. I try to peer back through the smoke of time, try to see him standing on the top of Mucklow's Hill, framed against the packhorse track, watching the gleaners in the fields below him, seeing the sunlight whet their scythes. I try to see the valley through his eyes, to see a scene little altered since the same sunlight glinted on the plumed helmets and burnished breastplates of the marching Roman legions . . . strange how the old ghosts walk the byroads of the mind . . . perhaps it's because they're not dead, after all. I wonder if that's what Graves was saying with his lines –

To bring the dead to life
Is no great magic.
Few are wholly dead:
Blow on a dead man's embers
And a live flame will start . . .

What was I really seeking here in the nature-stillness of woods and fields, I found myself asking. Was it just a holiday, a selfish opportunity to shun domestic responsibilities for a while? Was it a desire to have my friends say, 'Ooh, I couldn't have done it. You're made of tougher material than me'? In days when I fooled around a lot in spending the coin of my youth I used to say that it wasn't too bad to wake up and ask, 'Where am I?'; but that it'd be a real shock to wake up and say 'Who am I?' Probably that's the trouble with most of us, we just don't know who we are. We only know ourselves through what other people tell us; we only see ourselves as if in a mirror.

'Without a dream a nation will perish.' An American President once said that – I think it was Truman. How right he was, whoever. The truest gleams of philosophy, of truth, always seem to come in short-snatched sentences. The words don't overflow, each word is dependent upon the other. The balance is neat and accurate, as accurate as the scales of Justice are reputed to be. Take one word away and the balance is lost, add but one more and verbosity conceals the truth. 'Without a dream a nation will perish'; and without a dream a man will perish also. He may not notice his own perishment coming about . . . he may live to old or young age and not know that he lacked a dream – he may be filled with self-satisfaction, a sense of pride because he is respected or admired or even envied amongst his peer group. But does he have a dream? A dream beyond his own garment of outward-showing personality . . . personality . . . *'persona'* . . . the Latin for mask? Do we have a dream, or do we just have a major fantasy which drives us on. Are we just play-acting amongst the toys of society, becoming as greedy as selfish children rampaging through the toyshops of the world. Where is the man and where is the dream . . . where is the light, and where is the shadow . . . ?

John Donne wrote the lines 'No man is an island entire unto himself . . .' Beautiful words, deeply expressed, written from the heart as well as the pen. But Donne was wrong, because every man *is* an island, and what every man-island must do is to build bridges of deep articulation from one island to the next. This is the urgent, pulsing message of Nature and the cosmic intelligence. I feel that if we don't build these bridges, mankind will not only expire long before the life of the solar system which houses him dies, but he will deserve to expire. Mankind is not immune from extinction . . . he must *earn* immortality of the soul, and not expect or demand it as a right. There can be no safety in numbers alone, only in the quality of the numbers.

101

Perhaps this is why I had backwatered myself for three months; to try to get to know my own confusions more openly, to find out whether I liked myself or was bored with myself. In between working, mixing with friends and sleeping I knew very little about myself. I was a stranger inside a labelled identity. So where did I belong in the scheme of things, if there was a scheme? I constantly asked myself how I could ever hope to learn. Me, with no education to speak of. Ex pit-worker, ex-iron-moulder, ex-navvy, ex-RAF, ex-policeman, ex-convict – just a long list of 'ex's'. I'd spent so much of my life leaving bits of myself in the 'exit' side doors that I hadn't had the sense or caution to heed the 'no entrance' signs. If I'd heeded the latter I wouldn't have used up so much precious energy in struggling through the former.

I read and reread the bits of scribblings I'd penned onto birch bark, wondering why I'd penned them, wondering what had prompted them; wondering what sense if any they made, and if they made sense was it merely a useless capsule form of sense that had no useful purpose beyond itself – just another form of milk-packet pictures. Where did it all begin? Where would it all end?

An ink-cap and birch-bark scribbling . . .

Time must *be the fastest form of energy there is because there is no 'Now', only future and past. Light* can't *be the fastest because it takes, for example, about 12 minutes for the light of the sun – 93 million miles away – to reach us at our 'fixed' earth location. So there is a 'light lag' of 12 minutes, a light lag carried on the vehicle of space. Yet even as the light of the sun reaches us after 12 minutes it is no longer* now *with us, and it's no longer* now *on the sun. The light is already in past time. Even as I say 'now' the word and the impulse to say it belongs to the past. So, I must argue from a confusion of ignorance that* TIME *is the fastest speed there is to man, nature or the cosmos. It is so fast that the future and the past are travelling at the same incredible speed. Everything, including*

Space, Tachyons and Light, is a passenger inside Time, and Time can't be measured and never will be. It is the identity of what men call God.

Why the hell should I have written *that*? It seemed to make sense when I wrote it down, but it doesn't make sense when I reread it. Who am I to attempt to measure knowledge and scientific insight against the great minds of science? Aye, I think – but who am I *not* so to measure? I am *me*, and there's only one me, and there will always be only one *me*. If in nothing else, I am unique in that alone. It was, after all, worth coming to the woods if only to discover that message, with all of its emphasis.

I let the thoughts go, as I all too often did. I hadn't the knowledge or the application to follow them through, I just headed for the nearest exit again. I took up my rifle and went on the hunt, filling tomorrow's cooking pot. Snuffing some small life out in order that I myself remain fit and healthy. Would it always be the same, I found myself thinking. Did evolution have something more satisfying awaiting us round the corner? Would man reach a state where he took life-nourishment from the very air he breathed, instead of from limb, flesh and tissue? Trees and plants feed from the earth and the air, giving back to the earth the richness of their discarded leaves and petals to form food for the earth to feed them on again. A constant recycling – would the quiet scheme ever apply to man?

I aimed, squeezed, and dropped a rabbit. Re-aimed, re-squeezed, and dropped another. For some reason the warm dead flesh felt alien to my hands, just for a moment, and then the feeling was gone. My stomach was already dictating to my brain how best to cook them.

'Man's an animal, me lover,' Old Konk repeated in my mind, 'only he don't like admitting it . . .'

Aye, man's an animal, but a thinking one. Whether or not that makes him superior to the other species, I don't know.

I've never had a conversation with a rabbit or a pigeon, a pheasant or a hare. Never exchanged words with a cat or a dog. I've no way of telling if they have thought processes like my own. I can only hope for my own ultimate sake that they don't, otherwise I'd probably starve myself to death. Everything around us has life, from the fly irritating our food to the elephant lumbering in a jungle. From the oyster to the mushroom. Every time we take a step across the ground we kill microscopic universes with our feet. There's no end to it. 'That's life, me lover,' says Konk. 'That's life – and that's what death's all about.'

Oh, for the sweet innocence of childhood; no matter the physical hardships that surrounded it, there was still an awesome wonder about it, an exciting mystery. The innocence is lost as we age, we become cynical instead of breathlessly inquiring. Who other than a child would go out of a summer's night, as I did, with a jamjar to catch glowworms, thinking I could hang them over my bed as a see-by light; who but a child would want to collect fishscales to sew on shirt and trousers and become a Pearly King? Who but a child could drink in a lovely insight experience by throwing cups of cold water onto the outside of windows on a deeply frosty morning to watch Jack Frost freeze the water and etch and mould it into ferns and scrolls? Only a child could watch a woman scrubbing her kitchen flagstones with a stiff-bristled brush and see faces smile out at him from the circles and whorls of soapsuds. Only a child could do such things, or want to, and be caught up in the magic wonderland of his own innocence. Leaving childhood behind is like getting out of a warm safe bed on a cold dismal morning.

Perhaps I was in a self-pitying mood sitting there by my campfire on an autumn evening, the early darkness peering over my shoulder as if it wanted to warm itself. Alone with myself, with thoughts for guests. Why had I come to the woods, I asked myself. Surely not because I was dared to by my friend? And not for the novelty, because I often took off on my own with tent and rucksack. I sat for a long time with hirch-hark writing pad and pigeon feather quill, waiting for word-warmth to appear. The wind had started to pluck at the fringe of my woods, and in the distance it was howling a low howl across the meadows. But I was physically warm enough with the fire in front of me, and the rest of me wrapped in woollen garments and cold-cheating anorak. No stars in the sky, only glowering blackness.

Then I knew why I had come to the woods. I had come to find the phoenix of myself rising from its own dead ashes. It was a year since I had 'died'. The thought of it seemed like a not-of-me complexity, and yet of me at the same time . . . like Lazarus I have died many times and many times come back to life of a sort, a life of going through motions, a puppet on circumstance's strings. For far, far too long I had been a mere emptiness. It hadn't been a spur-of-the-moment decision, I'd known for a long time with increasing awareness what I must do. Pull out the plug, turn off the switch: but someone interfered, pushed back the plug, turned on the switch again . . . I remember waking up with a line from Sassoon chanting through a groove in my mind – 'No, not that way . . . not that way . . .'

The mind's an amazing thing, the way it speaks inside you.

I'd had enough of life, but especially enough of *me*. I'd lived half a century too long, I was worn out with a sense of uselessness. I had nothing to give of myself . . . I was an atom-bomb-blasted wilderness where nothing grew, nor ever would. I'd wanted 'out'. I'd left my wife and son, and my stepson, particularly my stepson. He was frail, physically and mentally crippled, dying slowly in my memory and my wife fading with him. I could not enter their world. I couldn't stay. I turned traitor; and in turning traitor fled from a situation which was bleeding me to death emotionally. I came to see the personal pain of recognizing loneliness in its present sense, the loneliness of self. From a distance, I loved. Loved my wife, my son, my helplessly lingering stepson. I loved many people and many things but from a distance, and the distance overtook me and put even further distance between

105

myself and me. I'd been going through motions, some applauded, some criticized; some fruitfully ambitious, some meaningless. I was the hollow man. And then I accepted my verdict and felt relief in the acceptance. It is only *now*, because of my woods, that I can see the perspective in the heart of things. At first there was a feeling of regret that interference took place, regret mixed with anger, resentment, in that such 'interference' was a violation of freedom to act against my own life . . .

. . . It was a Monday and I said that I was going into London to see my agent. I said I'd drive to the railway station, park the car, and then go on to London by train.

But I didn't. I drove into quiet woods and wrote letters to my wife and son, and one to the police. With me I'd got a lethal amount of tablets, enough to put three people down, I was told afterwards. I posted the letters to arrive next morning so that the police would find me before any out-of-school children came exploring the woods. I washed the tablets down with a quart bottle of vodka and sat in the warmth of the car. I felt calm and peaceful, as if I were listening to good music. I remember the night-darkness of the woods with a sliver of moon lifting over the trees. I remember thinking it was a poacher's moon, one which gave just enough light to see by but not enough to *be* seen. It was a deeply happy few minutes of conscious aloneness I experienced. No sadness, no regrets, just a feeling that a calm passage into sleep had come my way. I remember those last moments so vividly, so clearly, so *happily*: it was like coming home, having known no home before. Then gradually everything slipped away, every tendril of thought and self let go into a great peacefulness. But just before I let go, I actually saw myself above my own body there in the car, looking down upon it. I felt no affinity towards the body that was now a discarded overcoat . . .

. . . But the single sperm seed which gave me my identity bequeathed me the tenacity to live, because I didn't die. Someone found me there in the woods by the slimmest chance and I woke from coma five days later. And now it's over. Death had its moment but chose not to choose; it passed me by for reasons of its own, leaving me for the time that It will select. It left me with new horizons to explore, and hopefully find that rekindled glow of excitement and purpose inside the kernel of the exploration. I want to live, now; and I want to erase that awful feeling of dying inside, bit by bit, day by day . . . that inner leprosy which so many of us suffer from.

And I want to rekindle love and friendship's glow for others whom I have betrayed . . . love, in all its many forms, is too precious a warmth to let die; it leaves no corpses which can be buried, no monument, no tombstone, no fixed place to return to so's to lay flowers. It just leaves scarred mental tissues, a feeling of long-ago sadness, a destroying sense of futility . . . but there may also be a sort of beauty in lost love – not *dead* love – if there be no malice. You can almost separate it from the now of things and put it inside its own picture frame, then store it away carefully.

That is why I had come to my woods. To find myself. I had come to the woods because I was afraid of man-made darknesses pressing in. I needed space to discover the ability to think for myself, no matter in how much of a simple fashion. I needed to find out how to talk with myself: I needed to re-open my eyes and find that enchantment which I glimpsed as a child, but which flew away too soon. I needed to find my place in life, not to be put into a compartment of life by others and circumstances.

I had come to the woods to meet myself.

That's all there was to it.

Yet what more could a man seek?

Eight

One night, unusually mild for the time of year, I slept out under the stars. An owl mourned at the moon, a distant farm dog answered it. I lay warm and contented looking up at the stars, feeling some close affinity with specks of light which spanned infinity . . . I saw the stars pulsing above me and I felt my moods change like colour slides being projected on a screen. First of all I felt affinity, and then a sensation of littleness as if I were a microbe under the vastness of it all. I felt time and space wash over me and was almost afraid. I felt the essence of my own intelligence become a tangible thing which I could see, yet I shrank it to the size of a micro-microspeck and closed my eyes to shut away the universe without, the sky and the stars. I sent my intelligence – the essential me – down to the soles of my feet and told it to look upwards. And it did so. It looked up at me and didn't 'see' muscles and tissues, bones and organs, flesh, arteries and nerves; the 'eyes' of my new awareness saw planets wheel-ing, saw ever-spreading galaxies of planets and stars and universes . . . I *saw* the universe within, and it was of the same awesome complexity and harmony as the cosmic universe without. I saw in myself the planets wheeling, the galaxies of infinity, all part of the same great order . . . for a small fraction of time I *had* entered the Second Meadow . . . stood on the threshold of some strange, personal eternity . . . But my First Meadow mind, conditioned and trained by the society to which I belonged, could not keep the understanding. Could not grow into it and expand with it. It touched the secret and then let go . . . and I felt regret and sadness because I knew that I had Second Meadow yearnings but only First Meadow articulation and abilities.

My thoughts remained in the First Meadow. I had wanted to disregard time as man measured it, but how could I? May be it was a wisp of woodsmoke, or the crackling and spitting of a damp log, but my thoughts jumped over the bygone years and came to a place where I was a nothingness, living down and out amongst other scarecrows. The black bats of the human race, scarce noticed by the masses. I found myself thinking that there was even a minus meadow, a pre-first meadow of existence. When I came out of prison such a long time ago I'd sat round campfires on city wastelands with my then peer group of unwashed half-men, the ghouls and the goblins, articulating emptiness; eyes blearing through smoke and cheap crude alcohol, the living eyes of the dead. In the far-flung shadows the ghost of human dignity went whimpering through the night. Christ sagged on His cross to increase His wounds and the ancient philosophers of old drank hemlock by the gallon. The sky was the Big Top and beneath it life was only a circus. There was candyfloss for the children, flags and streamers for the patriotic, juke boxes for the dancers, dociled animals for the affectionate, towers for the poets and the dreamers, soft lights for the lovers, fortune-tellers for the superstitious and the religious; high-speed motion for the escapists, coconut shies for the resentful, danger for the proxy-sharers, soap-boxes and megaphones for the orators, boxers and wrestlers for the prejudiced and the spiteful . . . glitter and neon and tinsel to hold back the dark for the frightened, hurdy-gurdy screams and laughter for happiness. And distorting mirrors in the house of freaks for the drunks and the lost and the damned and the hopeless, the inadequates and the peram-bulating dead. Somewhere, out in space and time, Mercy itself stood poised to cut the guyropes to send the Big Top crashing down. A toadstool less in place and eternity.

I looked at the wrecks of which I was one, knowing that it was a coin's flip between right and wrong. If we'd been young healthy men camping out in the hills, we'd have been admired. As we were, we were garbage with no dustbin available to put us in. Perhaps, then, no matter how drunk we were, we puzzled at the stars, with our fragmented minds groping like spastic fingers for knowledge, for insight. Perhaps we each saw childhood painted on the stars, our own formative years which were never completed except in deformity . . .

But the past had gone away. I was no longer a bum on a wasteland, I was a me lying out in the woods under the stars, listening to the music of the spheres. Asking my mind what responsibility I owed myself. I was lucky. Back there in the bustling world people were milling around yelling out for freedom of speech while they lacked freedom of thought. Maybe Chamfort was right, I thought: 'Passions make men live, Wisdom makes them last.' I'd had my passions – was wisdom round the corner? Had my woods taught me the simple truth that hope is a good alarm clock to waken to, and faith a good pillow to sleep on? And what was faith, anyway? Had I conceived any inkling of it, beneath the levels of my consciousness? The danger in me had never been the tendency to put all my eggs in one basket, but to put too many baskets round one egg. I'd preened myself with small successes, measuring the success by the size of the payment cheque. Yet, in the final analysis, I was coming to the point of learning that I'd actually received payment for my own infant mortality rate of ideas. Vanity had all too often paralysed my deep-down creativity which I dared to know existed. I knew quite suddenly in a flash of blinding insight that I'd allowed well-formed memory functions to pose as originality. Crash! A sudden clenched fist of recall: a poem I'd read, thought 'pretty', and dismissed. But it had anchored into my unconscious and now, years after reading it, the words flooded back to me . . .

I bargained with Life for a penny
And Life would pay no more,
No matter how, at evening,
I counted my scanty score.
For Life is a just employer
And gives you what you ask,
But once you have named the wages,
Why, you must bear the task;
I bargained with Life for a penny
Only to learn, dismayed,
That any *wage I had asked of Life*
Life would have willingly paid.

'Wage' didn't necessarily mean money. Money was a by-product. There had to be more to a man than being a mere savings account, a walking, breathing chequebook.

'That's the road on't, me lover,' Konk said to me, as a bright moon wrote peace across the heavens. 'There's more to life than fags and shags, chap. Only the buggers who dictate our lives won't let us look up at the horizon . . . we'n got to keep our eyes on the ground where the bread and butter bist . . . somebody stole my mind an' opportunities when I weren't a-looking . . . somebody stole my freedom . . . somebody put me in an everlasting prison until I died. Not for thee, chap – get out'n it . . .'

The three meadows, stretching before me as I looked from my tent, gradually gave me a sharpness of mind I'd never experienced before. Other people might have done, but never me. The meadows were symbols of inner acres of knowledge, wisdom and experience. Gone away from me was the noise and bustle of ordinary living, the whine and roar of street traffic, the petty irritations of routine life. The values that I'd held dear in the years behind me suddenly seemed remote and of no importance – rivalries in commercial advancement, the daily clock-urgencies of appointments to be kept and tasks to be done. Suddenly these seemed to have no importance and no value.

112

The weeks had passed and I hadn't spoken to a single human being, not read a newspaper and not listened to a radio set. The only value I missed was that of music. Beethoven, Mozart, Vivaldi – I had to switch into my mind to give me music. Sometimes I walked the woods and meadows shouting music – in an unmusical manner – at the top of my voice. I found myself talking to the birds and creatures in Hiawatha fashion, talking to the early morning mists, the trees, the sky, the earth. It struck me that if I did the same things back in the ordinary world I'd get myself shut up inside a psychiatric ward, or arrested for being drunk and disorderly. In the ordinary world you speak to people, perhaps to pets, but not to Nature. She, who says so much, is seldom spoken to direct. She is third person, a distant Third Meadow. She's spoken to, or echoed in, paintings, music, art of man-made forms – she's hung on walls and admired.

But you have a *real* conversation with her when you can say aloud, unselfconsciously, 'Good morning, world', 'Good morning, mist and sun and wind . . .'

'Goodnight, stars and moon . . .'

But after the joy and pleasure of sharing this, the contradiction. The almost-hypocrisy: the necessary betrayal. To feel the stirrings of stomach hunger, aim the rifle and terminate a small life. Destroy a miniature universe, a microgalaxy. Pick up the dead pigeon and see the tantalizing sheens of blues and greens in the neckruff; colours which appear and disappear as you turn the bird against the light. Spread the wings to full span and see the same floating colours, the magnificent architecture of feather and bone structure. Feel the strong, light graceful curve of the breastkeel – over how many millions of years did Nature evolve such perfection, and for what ultimate purpose? Now dead and useless except to serve as protein in another species' system. A larger galaxy swallowing a smaller one – and what galaxy will finally swallow me? We are back once more with the powdered-milk packet.

And Old Konk's voice comes whispering across the winds of the mind: 'If God made man, me lover, He gave man the fish to tekken from the sea, the birds and fowl from the air, the beasts from the fields . . . it's life, me chap, is death . . .'

Solemn thoughts come pressing in; not morbid thoughts, but solemn – perhaps responsible. Here am I, cut off from the social intercourses of mankind. Here I am, bearded and shaggy-haired, with no instant press-button entertainment, no pubs, no TV, no laughing, agreeable or quarrelsome conversations except it be the quarrelsome complaints of the crows. Behind me are the trappings and wrappings of 'successes' like house, car, playthings. Good suits and a comfortable bed. A well-laid garden, food carried from kitchen to dining room, amicable friends. But they are transient. The success-things are not mine to keep. They are on loan to me only until the arrival of my death. I acquired these things in First Meadow existence, and I cannot prevent a certain sadness of mind which tells me I shall also relinquish them in the First Meadow.

Did that anonymous madman who died four hundred years or so ago feel the same when he wrote the lines which constantly haunt me . . .

And of your five sweet senses
may you never be forsaken,
nor wander from yourselves with Tom
abroad, to beg your bacon.

With an heart of furious fancies,
  Whereof I am commander:
    With a burning spear,
    And a horse of air,
To the wilderness I wander.

I sit here looking out on the English landscape I love so well, desperately wanting to pass out and into that Second Meadow of thought and feelings: the Second Meadow of spiritual experience which I know exists, but I cannot find the gate. I am a simple man, uneducated, unintellectual and without social refinements – and I feel cheated. Half-remembered lines from Kipling spill into my mind, lines he wrote on behalf of the soldiers in the Great War, that war to end all wars . . .

If any questioned why we died
Tell them, because our fathers lied . . .

And I feel an affinity with the dead soldiers who spoke through Kipling's mouth – did my fathers also lie to me? Have they taught me to put emphasis upon the wrong values? Has their collective training of me down the centuries – moral, educational, political – imprisoned me forever inside the First Meadow which is, after all, only a fenced-in paddock. Have they, to me no less than to Kipling's soldiers, lied by word of mouth, act, deed, and above all by the examples they set for me to follow? Have they brain-washed me into believing that First Meadow experience is the one and only? Was John Donne agreeing or warning when he wrote –

We are all conceived in Close Prison; in our mother's wombs we are close prisoners all; when we are born, we are born into the liberty of the house; prisoners still though within larger walls: and then all our life is but a going out to the place of execution, to death.

Was Beethoven mourning with us all when he wrote that second movement of his Seventh Symphony, or was he calling us from a Second Meadow or a Third to make the attempt and join him?

And what did Christ mean when, being flattered by men for His works, He turned aside their praise by simply saying, 'All these things that I do you too can do . . . *only even more so.*' He *must* have been calling from a Second or Third Meadow, mustn't He? If not, what's it all about? What the purpose and what the use of human existence? Why did one sperm seed become *me*? One seed out of millions, one single seed which carried *my* identity. Did it reach the sun-egg by random chance or by preplanned design of Nature, the great cosmic intelligence?

One thing is for sure. My short-long three months of aloneness has shown me that I am no longer content with the self or world I must return to. I have to go back, but I do not want to. I have walked and talked with some strange elemental force which puzzles but beckons me. I have sipped at the stars. They have made me restless with resistance – I am no longer satisfied with myself as I was. I have been geared to a vast machine. I have been a state slave, a number in a computer. I have been one of Donne's prisoners, inside increasingly larger walls . . . but still walls.

I want to be free. Inside my mind – I want to walk inside the Second Meadow of my mind and find true truths, not placebo clichés which masquerade as truths.

I have now experienced my first truly conflicting thoughts; the conflict lies in my own self-dissatisfaction. I have seen through patches of my own artificial ego, my own self-pretences, my own frailties which I thought were strengths. My thought conflict goes in search of peace, not war. The war of self, or the war of others. A Second Meadow of inner life draws me like a magnet. I *know* it's there, I just have to find the gate that will let me enter – it has nothing to do with 'man-made' religions: nothing to do with the icons of alabaster crucifixions and strange, jealous, vengeful gods . . . nothing to do with pulpit dronings, empty pomps and ceremonies. My Second Meadow has nothing to do with these man-made spiritual prisons, the dusty, gloomy, age-damp prisons . . .

The woods and meadows in which I have dwelled for a mere three months have told me I was born free, and free I must be. That freedom must exist inside my mind, the Second Meadow beckons there.

When I finally, reluctantly, came away from my campsite overlooking the three meadows it was the last day of the last week in November. Sky and landscape were winter-brooding, the wet grey mists haunted the woods and fields. The woods had been my home, my ghost would linger there because with them I had found many new and strange moods. As I folded my pup-tent and collected my few belongings I felt an urge that was almost an ache not to leave that place. I no longer wanted to return to the First Meadow world which after all wasn't a meadow but merely, as Donne had said, 'the liberty of the house'. Even the thought of reunion with friends and family didn't remove the feelings of sadness that I had to leave this place.

I left everything tidy, filled in the latrine trenches and grease pit, scattered the dead ashes of my many campfires to serve as compost, checked the stream to make sure I'd left no safety pins or wire hooks to endanger wild life. I'd collected in my rabbit traps the day before.

Would the wind and trees and night wonder where I'd gone, I asked myself; would they remember me, as I'd remember them?

I shouldered my belongings and left the calmness of my woods, walked across each meadow, shutting the gates behind me. Over the fields and down the winding lane to where I'd left my car in the village garage. The battery was charged up, the car ready and waiting. I stowed my gear in the boot, switched on the ignition . . . smelled the pollution of acrid exhaust fumes.

From the top of a hill I stopped for a moment and looked down on the woods which had sheltered me, at the meadows stretched in front of them. The November mists were already taking them from me.

Soon, I was riding the three-laned motorway towards London. Around me, big cars, little cars, coaches, lorries. Going north, going south . . . going somewhere.

The concrete roads stretched endlessly ahead and to rear, like punctuation marks from chapters of the future. First Meadow future, and no more than that. Future of plastic, concrete, hustle and bustle; future of income-tax returns,

rates demands, morbid world news from radio and TV sets
. . . unsmiling faces in city streets . . .

And when I returned home and took up the stitches of old
routines, I found that my three months of absence soon
receded into memory, almost as if they'd never been. The
memories of the woods and meadows seemed like cinema
memories – looked at, enjoyed, then half forgotten: eclipsed
by the pressures of here and now.

Yet still Old Konk's ghost voice and ghost companionship
lingered. 'Cull thee memory, boy. Cull thee memory – trust
thee memory to keep the truth on it all.'

'Aye, Konk,' my thoughts answered back, 'I know what
you mean. I've not left my Second Meadow behind, I've got
it here inside me – and I'll tell you this. One day I shall go
back to it and explore it in full, and then go out and find the
Third Meadow for sure.'